AQA

REVISE AQA GCSE
French

REVISION WORKBOOK

Series Consultant: Harry Smith

Author: Stuart Glover

Also available to support your revision:

Revise GCSE Study Skills Guide   9781447967071

The **Revise GCSE Study Skills Guide** is full of tried-and-trusted hints and tips for how to learn more effectively. It gives you techniques to help you achieve your best – throughout your GCSE studies and beyond!

Revise GCSE Revision Planner   9781447967828

The **Revise GCSE Revision Planner** helps you to plan and organise your time, step-by-step, throughout your GCSE revision. Use this book and wall chart to mastermind your revision.

For the full range of Pearson revision titles across GCSE, BTEC and AS Level visit:

www.pearsonschools.co.uk/revise

ALWAYS LEARNING   **PEARSON**

Contents

Audio files

Audio files for the listening exercises in this book can be found at:
www.pearsonschools.co.uk/mflrevisionaudio

A small bit of small print

AQA publishes Sample Assessment Material and the Specification on its website. This is the official content and this book should be used in conjunction with it. The questions in this book have been written to help you practise what you have learned in your revision. Remember: the real exam questions may not look like this.

Target grades

Target grades are quoted in this book for some of the questions. Students targeting this grade should be aiming to get some of the marks available. Students targeting a higher grade should be aiming to get all of the marks available.

Birthdays

1 What date?

Look at the dates of these events.

Le concert se passe le lundi cinq mai.	**Il y a une fête jeudi vingt-huit juin.**	**Mon anniversaire, c'est le lundi douze avril.**
Rendez-vous mercredi trente-et-un juillet.	**Il y a un festival dimanche vingt-deux mai.**	**Nous avons une boum mardi quinze août.**

Which of the following dates are mentioned above? Write the correct **five** letters in the boxes.

A	Tuesday 15th July	**F**	Sunday 22nd July
B	Sunday 22nd May	**G**	Monday 5th May
C	Wednesday 15th May	**H**	Wednesday 31st December
D	Wednesday 31st July	**I**	Thursday 28th June
E	Tuesday 15th August	**J**	Monday 12th April

Example: ☐ B

☐ *(1 mark)*   ☐ *(1 mark)*   ☐ *(1 mark)*   ☐ *(1 mark)*   ☐ *(1 mark)*

2 My cousin

Audio files
Audio files can be found at:
www.pearsonschools.co.uk/mflrevisionaudio

> Make sure you know the French alphabet. You must get every letter of this name correct to earn one mark.

Listen to these details about Janine's cousin.

Fill in the details **in English**.

Example: First name   .... *Lucie* ....

Part 1

(a) Family name   ....   *(1 mark)*

(b) Day and month of birth   ....   *(1 mark)*

Part 2

(c) Born in   ....   *(1 mark)*

(d) Likes   ....   *(1 mark)*

Part 3

(e) Last week's activity   ....   *(1 mark)*

(f) Next weekend's activity   ....   *(1 mark)*

Pets

3 Talking about pets

Look at these pets.

A

B

C

D

E

F

G

H

Which pet is being discussed? Write the correct letter in each box.

Example: J'ai un hamster blanc que j'adore.   H

(a) Je voudrais un cheval noir.   ☐   *(1 mark)*

(b) J'ai un petit chien blanc adorable.   ☐   *(1 mark)*

(c) Mon petit lapin gris s'appelle Alain.   ☐   *(1 mark)*

(d) Mon frère a une souris grise que je n'aime pas.   ☐   *(1 mark)*

> Make sure you look for the **key words** in these sentences.

4 Opinions of pets

Listen to these young people talking about pets. What are their opinions? Write **P** (positive), **N** (negative) or **P/N** (both positive and negative) in each box.

Example: P/N

1 ☐   *(1 mark)*

2 ☐   *(1 mark)*

3 ☐   *(1 mark)*

4 ☐   *(1 mark)*

Physical description

5 What do they look like?

Look at these pictures of family members and friends.

A   B    C

D    E    F

> When you look at a picture, try to work out the French for the things you can see. This helps you to prepare for what you are about to read or hear.

Which description goes with each picture? Write the correct letter in each box.

Example: Son amie a de longs cheveux marron et un petit nez.   **F**

(a) Mon père est grand et a une moustache. ☐ *(1 mark)*

(b) Notre oncle Pierrot est assez grand. Il a de longs cheveux noirs. ☐ *(1 mark)*

(c) Ma mère est très grande et elle a les cheveux courts. ☐ *(1 mark)*

(d) Sa sœur est petite. Elle porte des lunettes marron. ☐ *(1 mark)*

6 My family's appearance

Pierre is describing his family.

Which feature is mentioned for which person?

A	B	C	D	E	F
hair	beard	body piercing	nose	glasses	feet

Listen and write the correct letter in each box.

Example: His brother   **C**

1 His father ☐ *(1 mark)*

2 His grandfather ☐ *(1 mark)*

3 Pierre ☐ *(1 mark)*

4 His mother ☐ *(1 mark)*

Personality

7 Carole's family

Read what Carole says about her family members.

> Mon petit frère s'appelle André. D'habitude, il est aimable, mais s'il est fatigué, il n'est pas très sympa. Ma sœur Danielle est toujours optimiste et elle s'entend bien avec toute la famille, sauf avec notre cousin, qui s'appelle Marc. Ma mère est un peu moins stricte que mon père, surtout quand nous sommes à table. Mais des fois, mon père peut être très amusant.

Which **four** statements are correct? Write the correct letters in the boxes.

A	Carole's younger brother is called André.
B	André is usually pleasant.
C	André is always pleasant.
D	Danielle is optimistic.
E	Danielle gets on well with the whole family.
F	Carole's mum is never strict.
G	At mealtimes, Carole's dad is as strict as her mum.
H	The family never sit around the meal table together.
I	Carole's dad is occasionally funny.

☐ *(1 mark)*   ☐ *(1 mark)*   ☐ *(1 mark)*   ☐ *(1 mark)*

8 The Delors family

Listen to Madame Delors talking about her family. How does she describe them? Write the correct letter in each box.

A	B	C	D	E	F
selfish	kind	hard-working	noisy	funny	lazy

Write the correct letter in each box.

Example: Nathan [E]

(a) Patrick   ☐   *(1 mark)*

(b) Martine   ☐   *(1 mark)*

(c) Sylvie   ☐   *(1 mark)*

(d) Jacques   ☐   *(1 mark)*

Brothers and sisters

9 Samir's email

Read this email from Samir.

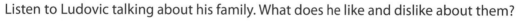

effacer   répondre   répondre à tous   avant   imprimer

Salut!

Je m'appelle Samir et j'habite près de Rennes avec ma famille, c'est-à-dire ma mère qui s'appelle Marianne, mes deux sœurs qui s'appellent Sunita et Laure, et notre adorable chien.

Sunita est plus jeune que moi et je m'entends très bien avec elle car elle est sociable et bavarde comme moi, mais Laure, qui est plus âgée que moi, m'énerve car elle m'énerve et nous nous disputons beaucoup.

Mes parents sont séparés et mon père habite à Limoges dans un petit appartement. Je m'entends bien avec ma mère car elle est toujours compréhensive, mais je vois mon père rarement, seulement une fois par mois quand je lui rends visite. Néanmoins j'aime bien aller chez lui, surtout parce que mon demi-frère Michel est vraiment sympa et nous aimons les mêmes choses. Par exemple, le mois dernier nous sommes allés à la pêche ensemble et nous nous sommes beaucoup amusés. Je peux lui parler de tout.

Read these statements. Write **T** (true), **F** (false) or **?** (not mentioned in the text) in each box.

Example: Samir lives in Rennes.   F

(a) Samir has an elder sister.   ☐   *(1 mark)*

(b) He gets on well with both of his sisters.   ☐   *(1 mark)*

(c) Samir lives in a big house.   ☐   *(1 mark)*

(d) Michel is older than Samir.   ☐   *(1 mark)*

(e) Samir and Michel both like fishing.   ☐   *(1 mark)*

(f) Michel loves the countryside.   ☐   *(1 mark)*

10 Ludovic's family

Listen to Ludovic talking about his family. What does he like and dislike about them?

A	is fun to play with
B	buys me treats
C	talks too much
D	is boring
E	doesn't talk to me
F	sometimes won't play with me

- Remember to listen for the subject of the verb when more than one person is being discussed. Note *je* (I), *il* (he) and *elle* (she) as well as any specific names.

- As usual, be careful to listen for negatives (*ne … pas*).

Write the correct letter in each box.

Example: Laura   E

(a) Nana ☐   *(1 mark)*   (c) Mickaël ☐   *(1 mark)*

(b) Mimi ☐   *(1 mark)*   (d) Céline ☐   *(1 mark)*

Family

11 Richard's family

Read what Richard says about his family.

> Je m'appelle Richard et j'habite dans un petit village pittoresque dans le sud de la France, pas loin de la côte. Avant, j'habitais une petite ville dans le sud-ouest de la France près de la frontière espagnole mais mon père a trouvé un nouvel emploi, donc on a dû déménager. Mon père, qui a quarante ans comme ma mère, travaille dans une usine comme ingénieur et il trouve son travail satisfaisant. Ma mère travaillait dans une banque mais elle est en train de chercher un emploi car elle a dû quitter son poste quand on est venu vivre ici.
>
> J'ai une sœur, Monique, qui est plus jeune que moi, et un frère jumeau, David, avec qui je m'entends fort bien car naturellement on aime les mêmes choses sauf qu'il aime le foot tandis que, moi, je préfère le rugby à quinze.
>
> Monique a eu des difficultés dans sa nouvelle école mais elle vient de trouver une copine, Alice, et elle est plus heureuse maintenant.

Which **five** statements are correct? Write the correct letters in the boxes.

A	Richard lives near the seaside.
B	Richard lives near Spain.
C	Richard's dad is older than his mum.
D	Richard's dad hates his job.
E	Richard's mum used to work in a bank.
F	Richard's mum now works at the station.
G	Richard's mum is currently unemployed.
H	Monique is older than Richard.
I	David is the same age as Richard.
J	David prefers rugby to football.
K	Monique has recently made a friend.

☐ *(1 mark)*   ☐ *(1 mark)*   ☐ *(1 mark)*   ☐ *(1 mark)*   ☐ *(1 mark)*

12 My complicated family

Listen to Bruno talking about his family.

Answer the following questions **in English**.

 Jot down notes in English or French while you are listening – but make sure your final answers are all written **in English**.

(a) How old was Bruno when his mother remarried? .... *(1 mark)*

(b) What **two** facts do we learn about his mother's new husband?

     (i) ....   **(ii)** .... *(2 marks)*

(c) Give **one** example of Bruno's bad behaviour. .... *(1 mark)*

(d) Where does Bruno's natural father live? .... *(1 mark)*

(e) How do Bruno's parents show they have confidence in him? .... *(1 mark)*

(f) How does Bruno now feel about his three parents, and why?

     (i) ....   **(ii)** .... *(2 marks)*

Friends

C

13 Talking about my friends

Read these comments about friendship.

> ## Quelles sont les qualités de tes ami(e)s?
>
> Mon amie **Maryse** ne refuse jamais d'aider ses amis.
>
> **Suzanne** est toujours prête à donner de l'argent aux personnes pauvres.
>
> Mon meilleur ami **Robert** aime bien écouter les avis de tout le monde.
>
> **Lola** essaie d'identifier une bonne qualité si on lui demande son avis sur un collègue.
>
> **Carla** n'est jamais de mauvaise humeur, même si elle est fatiguée.

Write the correct name next to each statement.

Example: Who values other people's opinions? ....Robert.............

(a) Who is never moody? .... *(1 mark)*

(b) Who is willing to give financial assistance? .... *(1 mark)*

(c) Who always says yes if a friend needs help? .... *(1 mark)*

(d) Who concentrates on people's strengths? .... *(1 mark)*

14 Gina's friends

Gina is talking about her friends. What are they like?

> Before listening, think of the French words for these adjectives.

A	B	C	D	E	F
fat	tall	pretty	small	medium height	thin

Listen and write the correct letter in each box.

Example: Zoë [B]

1 Christophe [ ] *(1 mark)*

2 Christina [ ] *(1 mark)*

3 Kevin [ ] *(1 mark)*

4 Marie [ ] *(1 mark)*

Daily routine

15 My morning routine

Read the following sentences and fill in the gaps **in English**.

Example: | Je me lève à sept heures et demie tous les jours. |

I get up at ....7:30........ every day.

> In questions like this on daily routine, if you don't know the answer, have a sensible guess. A suitable time, place or activity could gain you the mark.

(a) | À sept heures quarante, je me douche. |

At 7.40, I .... *(1 mark)*

(b) | Je prends le petit déjeuner dans la cuisine. |

I have breakfast in the .... *(1 mark)*

(c) | Je quitte la maison à huit heures et quart. |

I leave home at .... *(1 mark)*

(d) | Je vais au collège à pied. |

I go to school .... *(1 mark)*

16 My routine

Listen to three young people talking about their routines. For each person, write an advantage and a disadvantage of their routine **in English**.

Example:	Advantage	Disadvantage
Sarah's morning routine	can do homework before lessons start	gets up too early

	Advantage	Disadvantage
Frank's evening meal		

(2 marks)

	Advantage	Disadvantage
Mélissa's weekend bedtime		

(2 marks)

Breakfast

17 Amandine's breakfast routine

Read what Amandine says about her breakfast routine.

> Je prends mon petit déjeuner à sept heures et quart. Je dois prendre le car de ramassage de huit heures parce que j'habite loin de mon collège. Moi, je n'aime pas les céréales, alors je mange tout simplement du pamplemousse, mais ma sœur préfère les crêpes. Comme boisson, je préfère prendre du thé car je déteste le café.

Read the following statements. Write **T** (true), **F** (false) or **?** (not mentioned in the text) in each box.

Example: Amandine gets up at 6.30.   ☐ **?**

(a) Amandine has breakfast at 7.15.   ☐   *(1 mark)*

(b) She travels to school by car.   ☐   *(1 mark)*

(c) She lives near her school.   ☐   *(1 mark)*

(d) She has grapefruit for breakfast.   ☐   *(1 mark)*

(e) She likes strawberries.   ☐   *(1 mark)*

(f) She drinks tea in the morning.   ☐   *(1 mark)*

18 What do they eat for breakfast?

Aline, Pierre and Bernadette are talking about their breakfast.

What do they eat and drink? Listen and write the correct letter in each box.

Example: In the morning, Aline has …

A	cereal.
B	a croissant.
C	bread and jam.

☐ **C**

(a) Aline drinks …

A	nothing.
B	milk.
C	water.

☐   *(1 mark)*

(b) On weekdays, Pierre drinks …

A	cold milk.
B	tea.
C	coffee.

☐   *(1 mark)*

(c) At the weekend, Pierre eats …

A	eggs.
B	a grapefruit.
C	a croissant.

☐   *(1 mark)*

(d) Before school, Bernadette eats …

A	nothing.
B	a ham sandwich.
C	only part of her breakfast.

☐   *(1 mark)*

Eating at home

19 A birthday celebration

Read Sylvestre's account of a meal at home.

> Je ne vais jamais oublier le repas extraordinaire que nous avons fait chez nous il y a un mois. C'était pour fêter les soixante-quinze ans de ma mère. Nous lui avions demandé si elle voulait bien inviter ses amis, mais elle a dit qu'elle pourrait trouver ça assez stressant et que son rhume n'était pas complètement parti.
>
> Mon père a tout préparé car il a voulu montrer à toute la famille qu'il était doué pour faire la cuisine et pensait que Maman méritait de se détendre le jour de son anniversaire. J'ai été très surpris par la qualité de ce que nous avons mangé, alors que ma sœur n'a rien aimé.
>
> Quand elle a compris que Papa avait préparé ce repas merveilleux, Maman a été très reconnaissante et a trouvé ça incroyable.
>
> Hier, elle m'a dit qu'elle espère qu'il va recommencer avec le repas de Noël!

> You don't need to write full sentences. Only give the answer needed. If you add more, you may give some wrong information and lose marks.

Answer the following questions **in English**.

(a) When was this special meal? .... *(1 mark)*

(b) Why didn't the mother want to invite lots of other guests? Give **two** reasons.

    (i) ....

    (ii) .... *(2 marks)*

(c) What did the father hope to do by cooking the birthday meal? Give **two** details.

    (i) ....

    (ii) .... *(2 marks)*

(d) What did Sylvestre's sister think of the meal? .... *(1 mark)*

(e) What was the mother's initial reaction when she realised who had cooked the meal? Give **two** details.

    (i) ....

    (ii) .... *(2 marks)*

20 Eating at home

What do they like to eat? Listen and fill in the gaps in **English**.

Example: Sophie likes ....*rice*...............

(a) Sophie does not like .... *(1 mark)*

(b) Emilie eats a lot of .... *(1 mark)*

(c) Emilie eats ....from time to time. *(1 mark)*

(d) Marc likes eating .... *(1 mark)*

Eating in a café

21 Eating out

Read this account of a family's visit to a café. Choose a word from the grid to fill each gap. Write the correct letter in each box.

Example: Hier, je suis allé à un ☐**L** en ville.

(a) J'ai pris un sandwich au fromage et j'ai ☐ une limonade. *(1 mark)*

(b) Mon frère a commandé la ☐ du jour mais elle n'était pas bonne. *(1 mark)*

(c) Ma sœur a choisi une salade ☐. *(1 mark)*

(d) Ma mère a décidé d' ☐ la tarte au citron. *(1 mark)*

(e) Mon père n'a ☐ mangé, mais il a commandé une bière. *(1 mark)*

(f) Le service était excellent, alors on a laissé un ☐. *(1 mark)*

(g) Nous allons bientôt ☐ retourner. *(1 mark)*

(h) Nous ☐ sommes très bien amusés. *(1 mark)*

> Remember that when the gap follows words such as *un*, *une*, *le*, *la* or *l'*, the missing word will probably be a noun.

A	baguette	I	soupe
B	essayer	J	aller
C	prendre	K	pourboire
D	rien	L	café
E	mangé	M	coca
F	verte	N	y
G	bu	O	en
H	rôti	P	nous

22 At the café

Listen to these people in a café. What are their opinions? Write **P** (positive), **N** (negative) or **P/N** (both positive and negative) in each box.

Example: Ice cream ☐ P

1 Chicken ☐ *(1 mark)*

2 Chips ☐ *(1 mark)*

3 Chocolate cake ☐ *(1 mark)*

4 Beef sandwich ☐ *(1 mark)*

Eating in a restaurant

23 Eating in a restaurant

Read what these three young people say about eating out.

> **Clément:** La semaine dernière, je suis allé à un restaurant italien en ville avec ma famille. On y est allés pour fêter l'anniversaire de mon frère et c'était une soirée géniale. J'ai choisi les fruits de mer avec des haricots verts et comme dessert j'ai pris un gâteau au chocolat.

> **Nina:** Je vais rarement au restaurant, mais il y a deux mois, j'ai mangé dans un petit restaurant chic avec mon petit ami. J'ai pris un steak délicieux avec des pommes de terre et des petits pois. La serveuse était très polie, alors nous avons laissé un gros pourboire.

> **Assiom:** Hier, j'ai mangé un plat traditionnel dans un restaurant français. Après avoir pris des escargots, j'ai essayé du poulet sans légumes, et pour terminer le repas j'ai mangé des cerises avec une glace à la vanille. Malheureusement, le service était nul!

Who says each of these statements? Write **C** (Clément), **N** (Nina) or **A** (Assiom) in each box.

Example: I went to an Italian restaurant.   `C`

(a) I had fruit for pudding.   ☐   *(1 mark)*

(b) I don't often eat out at a restaurant.   ☐   *(1 mark)*

(c) I ate the seafood.   ☐   *(1 mark)*

(d) The service was really good.   ☐   *(1 mark)*

(e) I went out with a friend.   ☐   *(1 mark)*

(f) I went out with a group of people.   ☐   *(1 mark)*

(g) I ate snails.   ☐   *(1 mark)*

(h) I did not eat any vegetables.   ☐   *(1 mark)*

24 Orders in a restaurant

Listen to these orders. Fill in the gaps **in English**.

Example: Sylvie likes .... fish ....

1 Pauline likes .... but hates ....   *(2 marks)*

2 Théo dislikes .... but really likes ....   *(2 marks)*

3 Jules likes .... but doesn't like ....   *(2 marks)*

4 Sonia loves .... but hates ....   *(2 marks)*

Healthy eating

25 Who eats what?

Read these people's views on sugar in food.

Vos avis sont importants!	
Michelle:	J'essaie de ne pas manger trop de sucreries.
Robert:	Je ne peux jamais résister aux plats sucrés.
Suzanne:	Trop de sucre, ça me donne mal au cœur.
Anne:	Les fraises sont meilleures si on met un peu de sucre dessus.
Ibrahim:	Le sucre, j'en ai horreur!
Pauline:	À mon avis, un peu de sucre ne fait pas de mal.
Roger:	C'est le médecin qui m'a dit de réduire la quantité de sucre que je mange.
Souad:	À mon avis, le café est meilleur sans sucre.
Benjamin:	Pour avoir de belles dents, n'exagérez pas avec le sucre!

Who says what? Write the correct name in each space in the grid.

Example: Coffee is better without sugar.	Souad	
(a) I have been advised to eat less sugar.		*(1 mark)*
(b) I can't stand sugar.		*(1 mark)*
(c) I think that a small amount of sugar does no harm.		*(1 mark)*
(d) I have difficulty saying no to sweet foods.		*(1 mark)*

26 Food choices

Listen to this girl talking about food. What reasons does she give to explain why the members of her family don't eat certain foods?

Write the correct letter in each box.

Example: Cheese | H |

(a) Mayonnaise ☐ *(1 mark)*

(b) Vegetables ☐ *(1 mark)*

(c) Grapefruit ☐ *(1 mark)*

(d) Chocolate ☐ *(1 mark)*

A	too acid
B	causes constipation
C	bad for the teeth
D	not enough vitamins
E	too much fat
F	too much sugar
G	not enough taste
H	has an allergy to it
I	often makes the person ill

Health issues

27 A healthy lifestyle

Read this article about Annie's attitude towards eating, drinking and smoking.

> Ce que je mange: je peux résister à tout, sauf à la tentation de manger du fromage même si je sais que c'est assez mauvais pour la santé. Le matin, je suis très pressée de partir au bureau, alors je n'ai que rarement le temps de prendre le petit déjeuner, ce qui ne fait pas plaisir à ma mère. Par contre, je mange assez sainement à midi car notre restaurant au travail propose tout un choix de salades et d'autres plats légers. Je ne suis pas végétarienne, mais j'essaie de limiter ma consommation de bœuf car un ami médecin m'a dit que ce n'est pas recommandé.
>
> Ce que je bois: je n'ai jamais eu envie de choisir des boissons alcoolisées, alors que presque tous mes amis en boivent depuis des années. Les boissons sucrées ne m'intéressent pas parce que j'ai envie de toujours avoir de belles dents, alors je bois beaucoup d'eau.
>
> Le tabac: l'un de mes meilleurs amis fume depuis quelques mois et j'ai envie de lui dire qu'il doit arrêter. Sinon, il va avoir une dépendance au tabac. Je sais qu'il aurait peur de prendre du poids si jamais il arrêtait de fumer. Cependant je sais que le tabac finira par avoir un effet négatif sur sa santé. Je vais lui en parler demain, même si ça l'énerve!

Answer the following questions **in English**.

Example: What food can Annie not resist? ....*cheese*............

> Take care when looking at tenses. Remember that *-ais* and *-ait* can be imperfect tense or conditional endings, so look back at the stem to be sure.

(a) Why does Annie not have breakfast?

.... *(1 mark)*

(b) Why does she think she eats healthily at lunchtime?

(i) .... **(ii)** .... *(2 marks)*

(c) Why does she try to limit the amount of beef she eats? .... *(1 mark)*

(d) Why does she not drink sugary drinks? .... *(1 mark)*

(e) She says her friend who smokes would be worried about something if he stopped smoking. What would he be worried about? .... *(1 mark)*

(f) What might his reaction be if she talks to him about it? .... *(1 mark)*

28 Health issues

Listen to Bernard talking about health problems. Decide which of these statements are true. Write the correct **four** letters in the boxes.

A	Bernard is 23 years old.	F	Bernard was in a nightclub a month ago.
B	Bernard started drinking alcohol when he was 10 years old.	G	Bernard was eating out last month.
C	Bernard has recently given up alcohol.	H	Bernard thinks he needs to lose weight.
D	Bernard has given up smoking.	I	Bernard took a tablet which made him sleepy.
E	Bernard thinks he should give up smoking.		

Example: A

☐ *(1 mark)*   ☐ *(1 mark)*   ☐ *(1 mark)*   ☐ *(1 mark)*

Health problems

29 Problems with smoking

Read this account of someone's problems with smoking.

> **(a)** Je fumais vingt cigarettes par jour et j'avais essayé d'arrêter de fumer sans succès.
>
> **(b)** Je toussais beaucoup et j'avais des douleurs partout.
>
> **(c)** J'ai commencé à fumer principalement pour me détendre.
>
> **(d)** Un jour, mon fils m'a regardé d'un air triste et il m'a parlé du tabac car il était inquiet.
>
> **(e)** L'année dernière, j'ai réussi à renoncer aux cigarettes.
>
> **(f)** Je ne suis plus en mauvaise santé et en plus, j'ai plus d'argent!

> In questions like this, it is important to read the whole of each part before trying to find the answer. For example, it is not enough to identify *fumer* (to smoke) in (a) because several answer options mention smoking.

Choose an English sentence from the grid to match each French sentence above. Write the correct letter in each box.

A	I managed to give up smoking.	E	I used to smoke 20 cigarettes a day.
B	I smoked to relax.	F	My son was worried.
C	I had health problems.	G	I thought I might take up drugs.
D	I am better off.	H	I copied other people's bad habits.

Example: (a) E

(b) ☐   *(1 mark)*   **(e)** ☐   *(1 mark)*

(c) ☐   *(1 mark)*   **(f)** ☐   *(1 mark)*

(d) ☐   *(1 mark)*

30 Drink problems

Listen to these three people's views on alcohol, then answer the questions in English.

Example: What sort of person is Paul? ....shy................

(a) Why does Paul drink? Give **two** reasons.

    (i) ....

    (ii) .... *(2 marks)*

(b) (i) Why does Janine drink? ....

    (ii) What is she afraid of? .... *(2 marks)*

(c) Give **three** reasons why Lucas does not drink alcohol.

    (i) ....

    (ii) ....

    (iii) .... *(3 marks)*

Relationship plans

31 Future plans

Read the views of these three young people on marriage.

> **Noémie:** Moi, je voudrais bien me marier un jour. J'ai un petit copain depuis deux ans et je suis très heureuse. Je ne sais pas si nous resterons ensemble à l'avenir mais je sais que je voudrais avoir deux enfants. Selon moi, le mariage est important.

> **Amélie:** Je ne veux pas me marier. Mes parents sont divorcés et ils m'ont montré un mauvais exemple. Quand j'étais plus jeune, ils se disputaient tout le temps, ce qui me rendait triste. Je pense qu'il serait mieux d'avoir un partenaire.

> **Léla:** Moi, je viens de tomber amoureuse d'un garçon que j'ai rencontré à une fête il y a un mois. Il a les mêmes goûts que moi et il est compréhensif. Dans le futur, je n'aimerais pas avoir d'enfants car je suis trop impatiente et je ne voudrais pas me marier.

Answer the following questions. Write **N** (Noémie), **A** (Amélie) or **L** (Léla) in each box.

Example: Who does not want to marry?   ☐ A

(a) Who has been in a long term relationship? ☐   *(1 mark)*

(b) Who does not want to have children? ☐   *(1 mark)*

(c) Who was sad when she was younger? ☐   *(1 mark)*

(d) Who has recently fallen in love? ☐   *(1 mark)*

(e) Who recently went to a party? ☐   *(1 mark)*

(f) Who is in favour of getting married? ☐   *(1 mark)*

32 Future relationships

Listen to the these young people talking about future relationships. Fill in the gaps **in English**.

Example: Aline thinks that ......*personality*...... is very important.

1 Léon would like to meet someone who is .... but thinks

that .... is not important.   *(2 marks)*

2 Marianne would like to meet someone who is .... but thinks

that .... is not important.   *(2 marks)*

3 Ruben would like to meet someone who is .... but thinks

that .... is not important.   *(2 marks)*

4 Chantelle would like to meet someone who is .... but does

not want to go out with someone who ....   *(2 marks)*

Social issues

33 Helping others

Read about what Delphine does.

> Delphine travaille pour une organisation caritative à Paris où elle habite depuis deux ans. L'organisation s'occupe des personnes sans domicile fixe dont il y a des centaines dans la capitale. Pour Delphine, il s'agit d'offrir aux gens sans logement de la soupe et du pain, et d'essayer de trouver des solutions à leurs problèmes. Elle travaille tous les jours sauf le dimanche et elle aime bien son emploi.
>
> La semaine dernière, elle est allée dans un grand magasin où le propriétaire offrait des sacs de couchage, des couvertures et du savon à l'organisation. Le weekend prochain elle va les donner aux pauvres dans les rues.
>
> Pour elle, le travail bénévole est super important et elle pense que c'est quelque chose que tout le monde peut faire.

Choose the correct ending for each sentence. Write the correct letter in each box.

Example: Delphine works for …

A	a charitable organisation.
B	a shop.
C	a supermarket.

☐ A

(a) Delphine …

A	has worked there for two years.
B	works with homeless people.
C	is looking for new lodgings.

☐ *(1 mark)*

(b) She …

A	also works in a bakery.
B	writes an agony aunt column.
C	helps to feed the needy.

☐ *(1 mark)*

(c) She works …

A	on Sundays.
B	six days a week.
C	every day.

☐ *(1 mark)*

(d) She …

A	recently picked up some free items.
B	recently gave some essentials to the poor.
C	has recently done her shopping.

☐ *(1 mark)*

(e) She believes that …

A	only some poeple can work for a charity.
B	anyone can do charity work.
C	her work is not important.

☐ *(1 mark)*

34 Jobs that help others

Listen. What job does each person do? Write the correct letter in each box below.

A	Works with animals	E	Works to help the world's poor
B	Helps young disadvantaged people	F	Helps the homeless
C	Works with sick people	G	Helps the unemployed
D	Helps old people	H	Helps to find supplies of clean water

Example: ☐ D

1 ☐ *(1 mark)*   **2** ☐ *(1 mark)*   **3** ☐ *(1 mark)*   **4** ☐ *(1 mark)*

Social problems

35 Newspaper reports

Read these extracts from French newspapers.

(a)
> Le chômage est devenu le plus grand problème en Europe.

(b)
> Le propriétaire d'une auberge de jeunesse a refusé une réservation à un jeune car il avait un nom africain.

(c)
> Une élève musulmane a été exclue car elle portait un foulard pendant un cours de dessin.

(d)
> Une manifestation a eu lieu hier pour protéger les droits de l'homme.

(e)
> La faim est un problème grave dans certains pays africains.

(f)
> Quelques jeunes ont été agressés dans les rues parisiennes.

Choose a topic from the grid to match each newspaper extract. Write the correct letter in each box.

A	Immigration policy	**E**	Religious differences
B	Hunger	**F**	Violent attacks
C	Homelessness	**G**	Unemployment
D	Human rights	**H**	Racism

Example: (a) [G]

(b) ☐ *(1 mark)*

(c) ☐ *(1 mark)*

(d) ☐ *(1 mark)*

(e) ☐ *(1 mark)*

(f) ☐ *(1 mark)*

36 Life in Senegal

Listen to Arinda talking about her life, then answer the questions **in English**.

Example: What does she say about her dad? .... *he is unemployed* ....

(a) What does she tell us about her mum? .... *(1 mark)*

(b) What is the biggest problem facing her family? .... *(1 mark)*

(c) What has her brother managed to do? .... *(1 mark)*

(d) How has a charity helped her school? .... *(1 mark)*

(e) What does Arinda think should be done in the future? .... *(1 mark)*

Hobbies

1 What do I like to do?

Read the following views about hobbies.

A
Nager, ça m'intéresse.

B
J'aime bien jouer sur mon ordinateur.

C
J'adore collectionner les timbres.

D
J'adore faire du cyclisme.

E
Faire les magasins, c'est fantastique!

F
Nous aimons beaucoup lire des magazines.

G
J'aime écouter de la musique.

H
Jouer aux échecs me plaît beaucoup.

I
Nous adorons chanter.

J
J'aime bien faire du patinage.

K
Je regarde la télé souvent.

L
Moi, j'aime bien aller au théâtre.

Which hobby is mentioned? Write the correct letter in each box.

Example: Collecting stamps   C

(a) Cycling ☐ *(1 mark)*   **(e)** Singing ☐ *(1 mark)*

(b) Swimming ☐ *(1 mark)*   **(f)** Shopping ☐ *(1 mark)*

(c) Reading ☐ *(1 mark)*   **(g)** Playing chess ☐ *(1 mark)*

(d) Playing on the computer ☐ *(1 mark)*   **(h)** Ice skating ☐ *(1 mark)*

2 My hobbies

Listen to these young people talking about how they spend their free time.

What does each person do? Write the correct letter in each box.

A	goes cycling	D	stays at home
B	plays an instrument	E	plays sport
C	listens to music	F	goes for walks

Example: Emma   B

1 Pierre ☐   *(1 mark)*

2 Lucy ☐   *(1 mark)*

3 Thomas ☐   *(1 mark)*

4 Juliette ☐   *(1 mark)*

Sport

3 A sports fan

Read this article about Stéphanie's sport routine.

> Je m'appelle Stéphanie et tous les sports m'intéressent.
>
> Je pense que le sport est bon pour la santé. Mais mon père n'est pas d'accord parce qu'il s'est fait très mal à la main pendant qu'il jouait au rugby la semaine dernière. Pendant l'hiver, je joue au rugby au collège, mais ce n'est pas mon sport favori.
>
> Ça fait plus de cinq ans que je fais de la natation. J'essaie d'y aller deux ou trois fois par semaine, mais je n'y vais pas si ma mère ne veut pas m'emmener à la piscine en voiture. Je n'y vais jamais en bus parce que je n'aime pas attendre à l'arrêt d'autobus. La plupart de mes amis aiment bien faire de la natation. Cependant ils sont tous un peu moins enthousiastes que moi!
>
> Si j'ai de bonnes notes aux examens en juin, je vais continuer mes études. Ma profession idéale, ce serait professeur d'EPS, mais je serais obligée de faire trois ans d'études universitaires pour y arriver. Sinon, j'aimerais bien devenir monitrice de ski. Par contre, j'apprécierais moins l'idée de travailler dans un centre sportif.

Choose the correct ending for each sentence. Write the correct letter in each box.

(a) Stéphanie's father …

A	will be playing rugby next week.
B	recently injured his hand.
C	has not played rugby for months.

☐
(1 mark)

(b) Swimming is a sport Stéphanie began …

A	two or three weeks ago.
B	more than a month ago.
C	over five years ago.

☐
(1 mark)

(c) If her mum can't drive her to the pool, Stéphanie …

A	doesn't go swimming.
B	visits one of her friends.
C	takes the bus to the pool.

☐
(1 mark)

(d) Stéphanie would really prefer to …

A	work in an office.
B	become a teacher.
C	train to be a skiing instructor.

☐
(1 mark)

4 Which sport?

Which sport do they like? Listen and write the correct letter in each box.

A	B	C	D	E	F
swimming	water skiing	football	sailing	ice skating	horse riding

Example: Annette **C**

1 Jacques ☐   *(1 mark)*   **3** Loïc ☐   *(1 mark)*

2 Maxine ☐   *(1 mark)*   **4** Manon ☐   *(1 mark)*

Going out

5 Excuses, excuses!

Patrick is inviting friends to go out. Read their replies to his invitation.

- Je suis désolée mais je dois promener le chien.
- Mes parents disent que je dois préparer le repas de ma sœur.
- Je suis malade aujourd'hui.
- Je dois faire mes devoirs.
- Je n'aurai pas mon argent de poche avant demain.
- Il va y avoir du brouillard ce soir.
- Je serai trop fatiguée pour y aller.
- Maman dit que je dois me coucher à neuf heures.
- Ce soir, je vais être obligée de garder mon frère.

Identify the excuses given. Write the correct **five** letters in the boxes.

A	I have to do my homework.
B	I'm feeling unwell.
C	I'll be at the cinema.
D	I need to look after my sister.
E	I need to look after my little brother.
F	The weather will be cold.
G	I don't get my pocket money until tomorrow.
H	I must walk the dog.

☐ *(1 mark)*   ☐ *(1 mark)*   ☐ *(1 mark)*   ☐ *(1 mark)*   ☐ *(1 mark)*

6 Where shall we go?

Listen to these young people inviting their friends out. Where do they suggest going?

A	B	C	D	E	F
sports centre	park	swimming pool	sports stadium	cinema	shopping centre

Write the correct letter in each box.

Example: Jacques [E]

1 Anna ☐ *(1 mark)*

2 Éric ☐ *(1 mark)*

3 Bella ☐ *(1 mark)*

4 Paul ☐ *(1 mark)*

Last weekend

7 What I did last weekend

Read these accounts of what people did at the weekend.

> **Akua:** Ma mère m'a déjà refusé la permission de sortir jusqu'à dix heures du soir, même pendant le weekend. Ce n'est pas juste! J'ai donc passé le weekend dernier à jouer avec ma nièce.

> **Lionel:** Dimanche dernier, je suis allé voir un film en ville et je suis rentré à dix heures et demie du soir et mes parents ne m'ont rien dit. Ils ne m'ont jamais refusé les sorties, sauf si j'avais un examen le lendemain.

> **Zinedine:** J'ai toujours adoré le weekend. Je ne refuse jamais la possibilité de sortir le samedi soir. J'ai pu sortir samedi dernier, mais j'ai été obligé de rentrer pour dix heures du soir, comme d'habitude.

> Be careful! Just because you spot a certain time of day in one of the texts, that may not mean it is the correct answer.

Answer these questions. Write **A** (Akua), **L** (Lionel) or **Z** (Zinedine) in each box.

Example: Who loves weekends? | Z |

(a) Who has most freedom in terms of social life?   ☐   *(1 mark)*

(b) Who needed to be back home by 10 p.m. last Saturday?   ☐   *(1 mark)*

(c) Who thinks arrangements are unfair?   ☐   *(1 mark)*

(d) Who accepts all offers to go out on Saturday?   ☐   *(1 mark)*

8 Did they have a good weekend?

Listen to Jules, Betty and Cyril talking about last weekend.

Who says the following? Write **J** (Jules), **B** (Betty) or **C** (Cyril) in each box.

Example: I went mountain biking. | J |

(a) I was paid to babysit.   ☐   *(1 mark)*

(b) I was more active on Saturday.   ☐   *(1 mark)*

(c) I had to walk home.   ☐   *(1 mark)*

(d) I enjoyed my evening.   ☐   *(1 mark)*

Television

G
READING

9 I would like to watch …

Look at these types of TV programmes.

A	B	C
dessin animé	documentaire	sport

D	E	F
jeu télévisé	film comique	série médicale

G	H	I
actualités	musique classique	film policier

> Start with the ones you can do most easily.

Example: Liliane would like to watch the rugby match. **C**

(a) Guillaume wants to watch a documentary. ☐ *(1 mark)*

(b) Valérie is interested in detective dramas. ☐ *(1 mark)*

(c) The young twins love watching cartoons. ☐ *(1 mark)*

(d) Gérard will watch a game show. ☐ *(1 mark)*

(e) Simone likes watching the news. ☐ *(1 mark)*

(f) Julie loves to watch comedies. ☐ *(1 mark)*

C
LISTENING
23

10 TV programmes

Listen to these people discussing TV programmes. What are their opinions? Write **P** (positive), **N** (negative) or **P/N** (both positive and negative) in each box.

Example: Benjamin **N**

1 Mani ☐ *(1 mark)*

2 Jasmine ☐ *(1 mark)*

3 André ☐ *(1 mark)*

4 Hélène ☐ *(1 mark)*

5 Paul ☐ *(1 mark)*

6 Yvonne ☐ *(1 mark)*

> To help with listening, make sure you can recognise the feminine forms of adjectives when you hear them, as well as the masculine forms. For example, the feminine form *ennuyeuse* sounds different from the masculine *ennuyeux*.

Cinema

11 At the cinema

Read the article.

Si vous aimez le cinéma, profitez donc de nos offres exceptionnelles pour le mois de janvier!

Tout le monde peut profiter de ces réductions! Mais n'hésitez pas trop avant de réserver des billets, car les places vont partir très vite.

Dans la salle de cinéma, n'oubliez pas d'être assis à votre place avant le commencement du film et d'éteindre votre portable. Nous vous en remercions d'avance.

Bien entendu, on invite les personnes de tous les âges à venir voir les films, mais pensez surtout aux jeunes enfants qui se fatiguent facilement et qui ont du mal à se concentrer surtout le soir.

Rappelez-vous également que nos chers clients peuvent garer gratuitement leur voiture en toute sécurité dans notre parking souterrain.

Answer the following questions **in English**.

(a) During January, who can take advantage of the reduced-price seats? .... *(1 mark)*

(b) Why exactly is early booking advised? .... *(1 mark)*

(c) What must spectators not forget to do, once in the screening room?

(i) ....   **(ii)** .... *(2 marks)*

(d) Give **two** reasons why bringing children to evening films may not be advisable.

(i) ....   **(ii)** .... *(2 marks)*

(e) Give **two** advantages of using the cinema's own car park.

(i) ....   **(ii)** .... *(2 marks)*

12 An interesting film

Listen to Romain talking about a film he has seen.

Choose a word or phrase to complete each sentence. Write the correct letter in each box.

(a) Romain saw the film in …

A	Britain.
B	Bruges.
C	Quebec.

	(1 mark)

(b) The film was …

A	sub-titled.
B	in black and white.
C	in English.

	(1 mark)

(c) The main character was the …

A	murderer.
B	victim.
C	town of Bruges.

	(1 mark)

(d) Romain liked the …

A	special effects.
B	scenery.
C	violence.

	(1 mark)

Music

13 The concert

Read this article about music.

When looking for clues, be careful not to focus on just a single word as this may lead you away from the correct answer.

Je m'appelle Adrienne et j'ai seize ans. Je trouve que la musique est géniale!

D'habitude, je ne peux pas aller aux concerts parce que ça coûte trop cher. Récemment, ma mère a dit oui et m'a acheté un billet car le concert en question n'allait pas finir trop tard le soir. Papa n'était pas d'accord!

La date du grand concert est arrivée. J'y suis allée avec deux amies qui vont de temps en temps aux concerts. (Elles aimeraient bien y aller plus souvent.) La soirée était fantastique car la chanteuse avait une très belle voix et elle a chanté pendant deux heures. Malheureusement, j'ai perdu tout mon argent.

Read these statements. Write **T** (true), **F** (false) or **?** (not mentioned in the text) in each box.

Example: Adrienne is 15 years old.   F

(a) Adrienne likes music.   *(1 mark)*

(b) She finds that concerts are too expensive.   *(1 mark)*

(c) The concert she went to finished very late.   *(1 mark)*

(d) Her friends had been to a concert the week before.   *(1 mark)*

(e) The singer had a nice voice.   *(1 mark)*

(f) Adrienne lost some of her money.   *(1 mark)*

14 Musical performers

Listen to these young people talking about music. Choose a picture to match each person and write the correct letter in each box.

Example:.   H

1 ☐   *(1 mark)*   **3** ☐   *(1 mark)*

2 ☐   *(1 mark)*   **4** ☐   *(1 mark)*

New technology

15 How I use my computer

Read this passage about Pierre's attitude towards new technology.

> Lorsque j'ai du temps libre en fin de soirée, j'essaie de m'asseoir devant mon ordinateur portable, sans avoir mes petits frères dans les pattes. Ils m'énervent de temps en temps. Je commence donc par contacter mes amis. La plupart d'entre eux habitent en banlieue parisienne comme moi, mais certains sont allés à l'étranger pour trouver des ouvertures professionnelles qui manquent chez nous.
>
> De temps en temps, je réussis à gagner un peu d'argent en utilisant Internet. Par exemple, j'ai déjà répondu à quelques sondages en ligne et j'ai reçu un peu d'argent chaque fois. On n'y gagne pas énormément, mais je trouve que c'est une bonne façon d'utiliser le temps. Je suis intéressé par tous les aspects de l'informatique, surtout les jeux. Si je pouvais en inventer, je voudrais en faire ma profession.
>
> Mais n'oublions pas que les ordinateurs peuvent créer aussi des problèmes. Déjà, je n'arrête pas de tomber sur des virus, ce qui peut me faire perdre pas mal de temps. C'est très embêtant. Je trouve de plus en plus difficile de protéger mes détails personnels quand j'utilise Internet, même pour m'amuser.

Which of these statements are true? Write the correct **four** letters in the boxes.

A	Pierre likes to escape from his brothers' company.
B	Some of Pierre's friends live abroad.
C	Pierre has managed to earn a little money by responding to surveys online.
D	Pierre is not interested in computer games.
E	Pierre has invented some internet games.
F	Pierre is aware of problems caused by computers.
G	Pierre has invented protection from viruses.
H	Pierre finds it hard to be secure online.

Example: A

☐ *(1 mark)*   ☐ *(1 mark)*   ☐ *(1 mark)*   ☐ *(1 mark)*

16 Mobile phones

Listen to these young people talking about how they use their mobile phones. Complete the sentences **in English**.

1 I use my mobile to .... *(1 mark)*

2 I prefer to use mine to .... *(1 mark)*

3 I use my phone to .... *(1 mark)*

4 I prefer to .... *(1 mark)*

> Before you listen, try to think of some French **verbs** for things you might use your mobile phone for. Then focus on spotting those verbs when you listen.

Internet language

17 Using the internet

Read these views on internet use.

- On peut acheter ses billets de train sur Internet avant de partir.
- Pour mes devoirs, Internet est très pratique.
- Sur Internet, les livres coûtent moins cher.
- Les parents doivent limiter le temps que leurs enfants passent sur Internet.
- Je n'imprime pas beaucoup de documents car c'est cher.
- À mon avis, mon frère passe trop de temps sur Internet.
- Les sondages sur Internet sont très populaires.
- Malheureusement, il n'y a pas d'Internet dans notre village.
- Je trouve que mon clavier est trop petit.

Which of the following statements are mentioned above? Write the correct **four** letters in the boxes.

A	It's cheaper to buy books on the internet.
B	You can chat to friends online.
C	The keyboard size is a problem.
D	People can steal your identity online.
E	Parents can use the internet easily.
F	The internet can help you with homework tasks.
G	It's expensive to do a lot of printing.
H	You can buy rail tickets before you travel.

Example: ☐ H   ☐ *(1 mark)*   ☐ *(1 mark)*   ☐ *(1 mark)*   ☐ *(1 mark)*

18 IT issues

Listen to what these young people say. Choose a picture to match each person and write the correct letters in each box.

A

B

C

D

E

F

G

Example: G

1 ☐ *(1 mark)*   **2** ☐ *(1 mark)*   **3** ☐ *(1 mark)*   **4** ☐ *(1 mark)*

Internet pros and cons

19 Advantages and disadvantages

Read Ruvimbo's account about the internet.

> La plupart du temps, je pense qu'Internet est une bonne chose parce que ça nous permet de faire plein de choses qui ne nous semblaient qu'un rêve quand j'avais dix ans. Une fois que j'aurai terminé mes devoirs, je passerai plus d'une heure à chercher des cadeaux sur Internet, sachant que je pourrai trouver les choses que je veux offrir à ma famille à Noël, mais je ne fais jamais de shopping après minuit. En plus, ça me coûterait peut-être plus cher de tout acheter dans les magasins. D'habitude, je réussis à tout commander avant le quinze décembre, mais cette année, il me manque l'argent nécessaire pour terminer mes achats car je ne suis jamais payée avant le vingt du mois.
>
> Tout à l'heure, je vais même pouvoir bavarder avec mes cousins au Ghana, sans avoir besoin d'utiliser le téléphone. Mais je vais me dépêcher car je dois éteindre l'ordinateur avant dix heures.
>
> Mais imaginez le sentiment d'horreur d'une de mes collègues le mois dernier! Elle vérifiait que son salaire était bien sur son compte bancaire et a vu que quelqu'un lui avait volé tout l'argent qu'il y avait sur son compte. Au début, la banque n'a pas voulu écouter ma collègue, disant qu'elle aurait dû mieux protéger ses détails personnels. La banque a mis trois semaines à remplacer l'argent volé et à vérifier qu'elle n'avait pas donné son mot de passe à une autre personne.

Read these statements. Write **T** (true), **F** (false) or **?** (not mentioned in the text) in each box.

Example: Ruvimbo thinks that the internet is a good thing.   T

(a) Ruvimbo will spend time shopping at 1 a.m.   ☐   *(1 mark)*

(b) Ruvimbo thinks that shop opening times are too restrictive.   ☐   *(1 mark)*

(c) She has bought all her Christmas presents before the 15th December this year.   ☐   *(1 mark)*

(d) She has to switch her computer off before 10 p.m.   ☐   *(1 mark)*

(e) One of her work colleagues had money stolen from her bank account.   ☐   *(1 mark)*

(f) The colleague's bank quickly sorted out the problem.   ☐   *(1 mark)*

20 Opinions of the internet

Listen to these young people talking about the internet. Choose an activity to match each person and write the correct letter in each box.

A	B	C	D
play games	spend too much time in front of the screen	give your personal details away	buy concert tickets

E	F	G	H
keep in contact with friends	help with schoolwork	find a job	find a girlfriend or boyfriend

Example: D

1 ☐ *(1 mark)*   2 ☐ *(1 mark)*   3 ☐ *(1 mark)*   4 ☐ *(1 mark)*

Shops

21 Which shop?

Choose a word from the grid to fill the gap in each sentence. Write the correct letter in each box.

Example: Quand j'ai D de fleurs, je vais chez le fleuriste.

(a) On vend des ⬚ à la pharmacie. *(1 mark)*

(b) Je viens d' ⬚ de la viande chez le boucher. *(1 mark)*

(c) Je vais chercher des bonbons à la ⬚ . *(1 mark)*

(d) J'ai acheté des ⬚ à la boucherie. *(1 mark)*

(e) Nous ⬚ au tabac pour acheter des cigares. *(1 mark)*

(f) On vend de ⬚ à l'hypermarché près de chez nous. *(1 mark)*

> In activities like this, look closely at the word before the gap as it can often give you a good clue as to the missing word. For example, *nous* before a gap means that you will be looking for the *nous* part of a verb, which usually ends in -*ons*.

A	tout	D	besoin	G	saucisses	J	allons
B	pains	E	médicaments	H	vendre	K	porc
C	confiserie	F	avons	I	acheter	L	chocolats

22 At the shops

Listen to these young people talking about shops.

Which shop are they going to and what do they want to buy? Write your answers **in English**.

	Shop	Item	
Example: Éric	supermarket	toys	
1 Lola			*(2 marks)*
2 Jacob			*(2 marks)*
3 Gaëlle			*(2 marks)*

Food shopping

23 I would like …

Look at these different foods that someone is going to buy.

A	trois kilos de pommes	**G**	une douzaine d'œufs
B	une boîte de sardines	**H**	500 grammes de fromage
C	trois pains	**I**	cinq tranches de jambon
D	quatre bananes	**J**	douze pêches
E	trois croissants	**K**	dix oranges
F	un kilo de carottes	**L**	un kilo de raisins

What types of food are mentioned?

Write the correct letter in each box.

Example: Carrots   F

(a) Bananas ☐   (1 mark)

(b) Cheese ☐   (1 mark)

(c) Bread ☐   (1 mark)

(d) Eggs ☐   (1 mark)

(e) Apples ☐   (1 mark)

(f) Grapes ☐   (1 mark)

24 At the supermarket

What does Nasir have to buy at the supermarket? Listen and write the correct **six** letters in the boxes.

A	ham	**H**	yoghurts
B	mushrooms	**I**	strawberries
C	flour	**J**	chicken
D	sugar	**K**	peaches
E	potatoes	**L**	grapes
F	apples	**M**	fish
G	mineral water	**N**	grapefruit

> Before listening, try to think of the French words for all the food and drink in the grid. This will make it easier for you to identify the correct items when you listen.

Example: I

☐ (1 mark)   ☐ (1 mark)   ☐ (1 mark)   ☐ (1 mark)   ☐ (1 mark)   ☐ (1 mark)

Shopping

25 Sarah's shopping trip

Read about Sarah's shopping trip.

> En général, je fais les magasins le weekend avec mon ami Robert. Samedi dernier, nous y sommes arrivés un peu après huit heures et demie car je voulais être en ville avant l'ouverture des magasins. Robert a passé beaucoup de temps à trouver une veste, mais finalement il en a acheté une dans le sixième magasin où nous sommes allés.
>
> Après avoir déjeuné, nous avons fait d'autres magasins parce que je voulais vraiment acheter un roman pour l'anniversaire de ma mère, mais sans succès. Deux heures plus tard, nous étions trop fatigués pour continuer nos achats. Alors, nous avons pris un thé dans un petit café. Après ça, il ne me restait que trente minutes pour trouver un cadeau pour ma mère.
>
> Malheureusement, c'était trop tard car le dernier bus de la journée n'allait pas nous attendre! Je n'ai pas envie de retourner en ville demain, mais je n'ai pas le choix.

Read these statements. Write **T** (true), **F** (false) or **?** (not mentioned in the text) in each box.

Example: Sarah usually goes shopping with her friend Robert. `T`

(a) Last Saturday, she arrived in town just before eight o'clock. ☐ *(1 mark)*

(b) Sarah wanted to be in town by the time the shops opened. ☐ *(1 mark)*

(c) Robert quickly found a new jacket. ☐ *(1 mark)*

(d) The shops were less crowded than usual. ☐ *(1 mark)*

(e) Sarah wanted to buy a book for her mother's birthday. ☐ *(1 mark)*

(f) The friends had a cup of coffee in town. ☐ *(1 mark)*

(g) They missed the last bus home. ☐ *(1 mark)*

(h) Sarah is looking forward to going back to town tomorrow. ☐ *(1 mark)*

26 Shopping lists

Listen to these people who are out shopping. What are they buying?

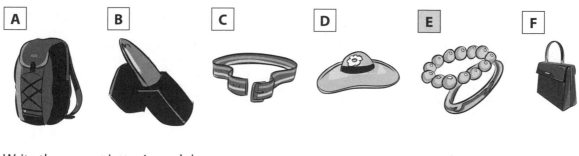

Write the correct letter in each box.

Example: `E`

1 ☐ *(1 mark)*   **2** ☐ *(1 mark)*   **3** ☐ *(1 mark)*   **4** ☐ *(1 mark)*

Clothes

27 Clothes and colours

Read these descriptions of clothes.

A	B	C	D	E
une jupe noire	un sweat rose	un pantalon bleu	un short vert	des sandales marron

F	G	H	I
une cravate rouge	des T-shirts blancs	un chemisier jaune	un pull multicolore

Who will buy what? Write the correct letter in each box.

Example: Ibrahim needs a new tie.   **F**

(a) Amadou is looking for a new pair of shorts. ☐   *(1 mark)*

(b) Aïcha would really like to find a skirt. ☐   *(1 mark)*

(c) Omar wants to buy a pair of sandals. ☐   *(1 mark)*

(d) Rahma needs new trousers for work. ☐   *(1 mark)*

28 Shopping for clothes

Patrick is out shopping. Complete each sentence by writing the correct letter in the box.

Example: Patrick wants to buy a …

A	shirt.
B	hat.
C	jumper.

A

(a) Patrick asks for …

A	large.
B	medium.
C	small.

☐   *(1 mark)*

(b) The first shirt he tries is …

A	too small.
B	much too big.
C	a little too big.

☐   *(1 mark)*

(c) Patrick finally chooses a shirt which is …

A	silk.
B	dark green.
C	light blue.

☐   *(1 mark)*

(d) He is pleased with the shirt because it is …

A	on special offer.
B	the last week it will be available.
C	his favourite colour.

☐   *(1 mark)*

Clothes shopping

29 Shopping advice

Read this advice on shopping for clothes.

> **Samuel:** Moi, j'ai tendance à éviter de faire les magasins de vêtements le samedi parce qu'ils sont trop fréquentés et il n'y a jamais assez de personnel! Si vous n'y êtes jamais allé en semaine, essayez d'y aller le mardi ou le mercredi car les vendeurs auront le temps de vous aider.

> **Béatrice:** Pendant les soldes, j'ai essayé de me trouver un nouveau manteau d'hiver. Comme d'habitude, j'ai été déçue parce qu'il ne restait plus que les grandes et les petites tailles. Rentrée à la maison, je n'étais vraiment pas contente parce que j'avais fait des économies d'argent pendant deux mois et puis ça faisait longtemps que je ne m'étais rien acheté.

> **Damien:** Si je fais les magasins à la recherche d'une paire de chaussures, je ne peux pas y aller sans ma soeur parce qu'elle a beaucoup de goût lorsqu'il s'agit d'être à la mode.

Answer these questions **in English**.

(a) Give **two** reasons why Samuel avoids shopping for clothes on Saturdays.

(i) .... (ii) .... *(2 marks)*

(b) According to Samuel, what is the advantage of shopping during the week?

.... *(1 mark)*

(c) What exactly was Béatrice hoping to buy? .... *(1 mark)*

(d) Why was Béatrice disappointed at the shops?

.... *(1 mark)*

(e) Why was Beatrice particularly annoyed on arriving home? Give **two** reasons.

(i) .... (ii) .... *(2 marks)*

(f) Why does Damien sometimes need his sister's help when shopping for shoes?

.... *(1 mark)*

30 In the dress shop

Zoë is trying on clothes. Her mother and sister Danielle are 'helping'.

Which of these statements are correct? Listen and write the correct **four** letters in the boxes.

A	Zoë quite likes the blouse.	**F**	Zoë says the striped dress is too big.
B	Zoë is in her school uniform.	**G**	Zoë doesn't like the colour of the jacket.
C	Zoë thinks the blouse makes her look very big.	**H**	Danielle thinks the jacket is too expensive.
D	Danielle thinks the blouse is old-fashioned.	**I**	Zoë's mum likes the blouse.
E	Zoë thinks the striped dress is pretty.		

Example: ☐ I

☐ *(1 mark)* ☐ *(1 mark)* ☐ *(1 mark)* ☐ *(1 mark)*

Returning items

31 Explaining what's wrong

Read the first half of each sentence and choose an ending from the grid. Write the correct letter in each box.

Example: Je voudrais être $\boxed{C}$

1	Ces deux chaussettes	☐	*(1 mark)*
2	Cette robe est trop	☐	*(1 mark)*
3	Maman pense que ma nouvelle jupe	☐	*(1 mark)*
4	Ce pantalon ne	☐	*(1 mark)*
5	Pour l'hiver,	☐	*(1 mark)*
6	Un imperméable rose et violet est	☐	*(1 mark)*
7	Les pulls à capuche ne	☐	*(1 mark)*
8	Je vais toujours au même magasin pour	☐	*(1 mark)*

A	me va pas très bien.	I	ont tort.
B	petit.	J	ridicule à mon avis.
C	remboursé.	K	je vais en acheter.
D	ne sont pas de la même taille.	L	sont plus à la mode.
E	est trop courte.	M	allons aux magasins.
F	grande.	N	mode.
G	pas assez large.	O	acheter des vêtements.
H	ce pull est trop léger.		

When you have matched up the sentence halves, read through your sentences again to check that they all make sense as well as being grammatically correct.

For example, sentence 1 needs a 3rd person verb (positive or negative). Choose your answer, then double-check it by reading the sentence again. Does it make sense?

32 Exchanging goods

Listen to this conversation in a shop.

Complete the sentences with a **word in English** or a **number**.

Example: The boy wants to exchange a .... T-shirt ....

(a) The first T-shirt is too .... for him.   *(1 mark)*

(b) He thinks the colour is ....   *(1 mark)*

(c) The T-shirt costs .... €.   *(1 mark)*

(d) The boy exchanges the T-shirt for a size ....   *(1 mark)*

Shopping preferences

33 What is important?

Read the following views on shopping.

Parlez-nous du shopping!

Jeannot: J'espère qu'il y aura beaucoup de choix au centre commercial car il y a plein de magasins là-bas.

Pierrot: J'aimerais garer ma voiture près des magasins car c'est pratique.

Madeleine: Je ferai du shopping quand il y aura peu de gens dans les magasins. C'est mieux comme ça.

Nadège: Trouver des vendeurs sympa pour moi, c'est très important.

Aline: Je préfère faire des achats sans quitter ma maison car c'est beaucoup moins cher.

Pascale: Le shopping? Ça m'est égal. Je n'ai pas de préférence. Des fois, je vais aux magasins mais j'utilise Internet aussi.

Luc: Je préfère ne pas utiliser ma carte de crédit.

Marcus: Je déteste faire la queue.

Who is discussing the following? Write the correct name beside each issue.

Example: Not queuing .... Marcus ....

(a) Crowd-free shopping .... *(1 mark)*

(b) Payment method .... *(1 mark)*

(c) Choice .... *(1 mark)*

(d) Shopping from home .... *(1 mark)*

(e) Shop staff .... *(1 mark)*

(f) Convenient parking .... *(1 mark)*

34 My favourite shops

Listen to Mimi and Janina talking about shopping.

Who says what? Write the **two** correct letters beside each name.

A	I like to get advice about books.	**E**	I like to try on clothes.
B	I like shopping in hypermarkets.	**F**	Shop assistants don't pester you.
C	I buy my shoes in a hypermarket.	**G**	I don't like shopping.
D	I go to the supermarket by bus.		

Example: Mimi: `B`

Mimi: ☐ ☐   *(2 marks)*

Janina: ☐ ☐   *(2 marks)*

Pocket money

35 Earning pocket money

How do the following young people earn pocket money? Choose a picture to match each person and write the correct letter in the box.

Example: Je fais du babysitting.   F

(a) Mes parents me donnent de l'argent de poche quand je range ma chambre.   ☐ *(1 mark)*

(b) Je gagne de l'argent de poche si je lave la voiture de mon père.   ☐ *(1 mark)*

(c) Ma mère me donne de l'argent de poche le weekend quand je fais du jardinage.   ☐ *(1 mark)*

(d) Je promène le chien, alors on me donne de l'argent de poche.   ☐ *(1 mark)*

36 Noémie's pocket money

Listen to Noémie talking about pocket money.

Complete each sentence by writing the correct letter in the box.

(a) Noémie usually gets her money …

A	on Sunday morning.
B	on Saturday afternoon.
C	on Sunday afternoon.

☐   *(1 mark)*

(b) She usually spends her money on …

A	presents.
B	clothes.
C	make-up.

☐   *(1 mark)*

(c) Last week, she spent her money on …

A	magazines.
B	a computer game.
C	make-up.

☐   *(1 mark)*

(d) She thinks her brother …

A	is very helpful.
B	gets too much pocket money.
C	doesn't save enough money.

☐   *(1 mark)*

Holiday destinations

37 Amélie's choice of holiday

Read Amélie's views on holiday destinations.

> Il n'y a rien de plus beau qu'un paysage couvert de neige.
>
> Mon dernier séjour à la montagne, c'était comme un beau rêve! Bien sûr, je n'aurais jamais pu résister à cette gentille invitation de partir la veille de Noël dans une station de ski. Mais on ne peut pas imaginer comme c'est cher de faire du ski! Déjà, la location d'un appartement, ça coûte pas mal d'argent. Puis, il ne faut pas oublier les skis qu'on doit louer, sauf si on décide d'en acheter.
>
> Je suis sûre que je vais être obligée de dépenser moins d'argent pour mes prochaines vacances. Alors, où est-ce que je vais partir cette année? Je n'en sais rien. Moi, passer mes vacances au bord de la mer en train de me bronzer? Ce qui est sûr, c'est que je m'y ennuierais énormément. Peut-être que j'aurai envie de passer une petite semaine tranquille à la campagne, car j'en ai marre de faire du tourisme dans les grandes villes.

Which statements are true? Write the correct **four** letters in the boxes.

A	Amélie thinks snow-covered landscapes are beautiful.	E	Well-located apartments are not expensive to rent.
B	The invitation to go skiing was refused by Amélie.	F	The next holiday will cost as much as Amélie's last one.
C	The ski trip departed before Christmas Day.	G	Amélie is not keen on beach holidays.
D	Skiing costs more than one imagines.	H	Amélie has already visited some major cities.

Example: A

☐ *(1 mark)*   ☐ *(1 mark)*   ☐ *(1 mark)*   ☐ *(1 mark)*

38 Holiday experiences

Listen to these people talking about their holidays.

What are their opinions? Write **P** (positive), **N** (negative) or **P/N** (both positive and negative) in each box.

Example: P

1 ☐   *(1 mark)*

2 ☐   *(1 mark)*

3 ☐   *(1 mark)*

4 ☐   *(1 mark)*

Holiday accommodation

G

39 Where are they going to stay?

Look at these types of holiday accommodation.

A	B	C
grand hôtel	auberge de jeunesse	à la montagne

D	E	F
terrain de camping	chalet	à la campagne

G	H	I
appartement	au bord de la mer	caravane

> Be careful not to confuse *camping* (camping) and *campagne* (countryside).

Choose the correct letter from above to match each tourist's choice.

Example: In a chalet `E`

(a) In the mountains ☐ *(1 mark)*

(b) In a large hotel ☐ *(1 mark)*

(c) At the seaside ☐ *(1 mark)*

(d) On a campsite ☐ *(1 mark)*

(e) In a youth hostel ☐ *(1 mark)*

(f) In a flat ☐ *(1 mark)*

C

40 How often do they stay there?

Decide how often the following people stay in each type of accommodation.

Listen and write **U** (usually), **S** (sometimes) or **N** (never) in each box.

Example: At home `U`

1 Campsite ☐ *(1 mark)*

2 Flat ☐ *(1 mark)*

3 Hotel ☐ *(1 mark)*

4 Youth hostel ☐ *(1 mark)*

5 Caravan ☐ *(1 mark)*

Booking accommodation

41 A letter of reservation

Read the following letter sent to a hotel.

> Madame / Monsieur,
>
> L'année dernière, nous avons passé des vacances très agréables chez vous, et nous aimerions réserver un autre séjour dans votre hôtel. J'ai décidé de vous écrire assez rapidement pour avoir les meilleures chambres.
>
> Auriez-vous la gentillesse de nous garder des chambres qui donnent sur la piscine, plutôt que sur la mer? Comme ça, nous pourrons surveiller nos enfants car ils ne demandent qu'à passer la plus grande partie de la journée à nager. Ça ne les intéresse pas de rester à l'intérieur.
>
> Cette fois-ci, nous n'allons pas réserver pour dix nuits comme l'année dernière car les dates de nos vols nous limitent à une semaine. Nous avons dû penser aux enfants qui auraient mal supporté l'idée des vols de nuit car ils se fatiguent facilement et ont tendance à se disputer!
>
> Nous attendons tous avec une certaine impatience l'occasion de nous détendre chez vous.
>
> Pierre Dubois

> Don't give too much information, but do make sure that you give enough!

Answer the following questions **in English**.

(a) Why are these tourists returning to the same hotel as last year?

.... *(1 mark)*

(b) Why is Pierre Dubois contacting the hotel so soon?

.... *(1 mark)*

(c) What choice of bedroom view does Pierre prefer?

.... *(1 mark)*

(d) What are the children not interested in doing on holiday?

.... *(1 mark)*

(e) How long will the family be staying at the hotel?

.... *(1 mark)*

(f) Give **two** reasons why they are avoiding night flights.

(i) .... **(ii)** .... *(2 marks)*

(g) What are all the members of the family looking forward to doing?

.... *(1 mark)*

42 Booking a room

What type of room does each person ask for? Listen and fill in the gaps **in English**.

Example: I'd like a room with a ....shower................

1 I'd like a ....room. *(1 mark)*

2 I'd like a Room with a .... *(1 mark)*

3 I'd like a ....room. *(1 mark)*

4 I'd like a room for .... *(1 mark)*

Staying in a hotel

43 What do you think of the hotel?

Read what these people say about a hotel where they stayed.

> **Que pensez-vous de l'hôtel?**
>
> **Marc:** Notre chambre était très propre, ce qui était plus important que le prix que nous avons payé.
>
> **Benjamin:** À mon avis, il y avait beaucoup de bruit, mais ma femme a très bien dormi, c'est l'essentiel!
>
> **Sophie:** Avec mes problèmes de dos, j'ai été contente d'avoir un lit confortable, mais la qualité des repas était notre vraie priorité.
>
> **Fatima:** On a opté pour un petit hôtel qui n'avait que quarante-cinq chambres parce que nous n'aimons plus les hôtels énormes.
>
> **Youssif:** Mes amis ont recommandé cet hôtel pour son restaurant, mais sa plus grande qualité, c'était son quartier calme.

> Beware of irrelevant material in the text, as this may distract you from the correct answer.

What aspect of the accommodation is considered the most important by each person? Write the correct letter in each box.

A	Neighbourhood	E	Sleep quality
B	Cleanliness	F	Number of bedrooms
C	Value for money	G	Personal recommendation
D	Food		

Example: Marc [B]

(a) Benjamin [ ] *(1 mark)*   **(c)** Fatima [ ] *(1 mark)*

(b) Sophie [ ] *(1 mark)*   **(d)** Youssif [ ] *(1 mark)*

> Remember that where more than one mark is available, you must give more than one answer to get full marks. But do not be tempted to give more than is needed – you could end up losing marks!

44 A recent holiday

Listen to this conversation about a hotel and answer the questions **in English**.

Example: Where is the hotel? .... in the south of France ....

(a) Why did the family choose this hotel and what did they hope to do every day?

(i) .... (ii) .... *(2 marks)*

(b) Why were the family pleased with the hotel? Give **two** details.

(i) .... (ii) .... *(2 marks)*

(c) What **two** problems did they have during the holiday?

(i) .... (ii) .... *(2 marks)*

Camping

45 At the campsite

Read what these three people say about camping.

> **Théo:** Je fais souvent du camping avec mes copains. Le weekend dernier, nous sommes allés dans le nord de la France dans un petit camping. Malheureusement, le bloc sanitaire était fermé et nous avons dû nous laver dans une rivière!

> **Marthe:** Moi, je n'ai jamais fait du camping, mais la semaine prochaine j'irai à la campagne avec ma sœur et nous avons réservé des places dans un grand camping. J'espère qu'il ne pleuvra pas! Je viens d'acheter un sac de couchage et une tente.

> **Catherine:** J'aime bien être en plein air, donc faire du camping me plaît énormément. Nous louons toujours des vélos et nous faisons aussi des randonnées. Le weekend prochain, je vais réserver un emplacement dans un énorme camping qui est situé au bord d'une rivière.

Which person is it? Write **T** (Théo), **M** (Marthe) or **C** (Catherine) in each box.

Example: Who likes the fresh air?　| C |

Who …

(a) has never been camping? 　　　　☐　　　　*(1 mark)*

(b) went camping last weekend? 　　　　☐　　　　*(1 mark)*

(c) likes to go for bike rides? 　　　　☐　　　　*(1 mark)*

(d) had to wash in a river? 　　　　☐　　　　*(1 mark)*

(e) has just bought some camping equipment? ☐　　*(1 mark)*

(f) mentions the weather? 　　　　☐　　　　*(1 mark)*

46 My camping holidays

Listen to Emma talking about her camping holidays.

What does she like about these holidays? What does she dislike? Write the correct **four** letters in the boxes.

A	being inside a tent
B	doing the washing-up
C	the colour of the tents
D	sharing with her sister
E	the beds
F	some of the meals
G	where the tents are pitched

	☺		☹	
Example:	C			
	☐	*(1 mark)*	☐	*(1 mark)*
	☐	*(1 mark)*	☐	*(1 mark)*

41

Holiday activities

47 Yvette's holiday

Read Yvette's opinions on things to do on holiday.

Which things does she **like** to do? Write the correct **four** letters in the boxes.

A	Je n'aime pas aller au cinéma.
B	Faire les magasins, c'est super.
C	Moi, j'aime bien faire du kayak.
D	Faire de la plongée sous-marine? Non, merci!
E	Aller à la pêche, c'est assez ennuyeux.
F	Jouer au volley, c'est mon activité favorite.
G	Moi, je déteste regarder les feux d'artifice.
H	Jouer au ping-pong, c'est une très bonne idée!

- Before you begin, jot down all the words and phrases you know for expressing positive and negative opinions. How many of them come up in A–H?

- Make sure you know lots of different ways to express opinions. This will help you in activities like this where you have to identify likes, dislikes and opinions.

☐ *(1 mark)*   ☐ *(1 mark)*   ☐ *(1 mark)*   ☐ *(1 mark)*

48 Going to a theme park

Listen to Luc's parents discussing going to a theme park.

Choose the correct ending for each sentence. Write the correct letter in each box.

Example: Luc will probably …

A	like the Cité de l'espace.
B	dislike the Cité de l'espace.
C	hate the Cité de l'espace.

A

(a) The Cité de l'espace is …

A	in the north.
B	too far away.
C	very close by.

☐ *(1 mark)*

(b) Luc …

A	likes long car journeys.
B	doesn't mind long car journeys.
C	hates long car journeys.

☐ *(1 mark)*

(c) The main problem with Futuroscope is …

A	it is too far to travel.
B	there is no cinema.
C	there are too many visitors.

☐ *(1 mark)*

(d) Luc's dad suggests visiting the Cité de l'espace …

A	in spring.
B	when the weather is very hot.
C	at the height of the tourist season.

☐ *(1 mark)*

(e) The final reason for choosing the Cité de l'espace is …

A	the price.
B	the facilities.
C	the transport.

☐ *(1 mark)*

Holiday preferences

49 Where would you like to go?

Read this article about two students' holiday preferences.

> **Pierre:** Moi, je serai très content de partir en vacances, après avoir terminé les examens de fin d'année. On ne pourra pas partir avant le dix juin car l'un de mes amis ne passera son dernier examen que le neuf. Puisque nous serons six à partir ensemble en vacances, il va falloir être d'accord sur notre choix de destination. Tous les autres veulent choisir la Grèce, alors que moi, je n'aurais jamais choisi un pays où il risque de faire trop chaud pour moi en été.

> **Marie:** L'idée de partir en vacances entre amis, ça ne m'intéresse pas. Dans trois mois, j'aurai vingt ans et je ne me sens pas pressée d'abandonner l'idée de partir en voyage avec mes deux sœurs aînées. La semaine prochaine, nous allons toutes les trois dans une agence de voyage pour réserver notre séjour de trois semaines au Maroc. Si on attend trop longtemps pour se décider, les prix vont peut-être augmenter, ce qui nous est déjà arrivé il y a deux ans. Ce serait dommage!

> Watch out for negatives, for example *ne … pas*. And be careful with *ne … que*, which looks like a negative but means 'only'!

Read these statements. Write **T** (true), **F** (false) or **?** (not mentioned in the text) in each box.

Example: Pierre will be happy to go on holiday.   T

(a) Pierre cannot go on holiday after the 10th June.   *(1 mark)*

(b) Pierre hates spending six weeks on holiday.   *(1 mark)*

(c) Pierre cannot agree with the others over their holiday destination.   *(1 mark)*

(d) Pierre fears that Greece might be too hot for him in summer.   *(1 mark)*

(e) Marie likes going on holiday with friends.   *(1 mark)*

(f) Marie is 20 years old.   *(1 mark)*

(g) Marie and her sisters are going to book a holiday next week.   *(1 mark)*

(h) Marie has never been to Morocco.   *(1 mark)*

50 What I like best

Listen to these young people talking about holidays.

What does each person like best? Write the correct letter in each box.

A	B	C	D
sunbathing	walking	sport	reading

E	F	G	H
staying in a luxury hotel	being in the fresh air	good weather	swimming in the sea

Example: C

1 ☐ *(1 mark)*   **2** ☐ *(1 mark)*   **3** ☐ *(1 mark)*   **4** ☐ *(1 mark)*

Holiday plans

51 Amadou's holiday plans

Read this email from Amadou about his plans.

○○○

effacer répondre répondre à tous avant imprimer

D'habitude, je passe mes vacances dans le sud-ouest de la France avec ma famille, mais l'année prochaine tout va changer parce que je passerai mes vacances avec mes copains. Il y aura des inconvénients bien sûr car mon père ne sera pas là pour tout payer et pour résoudre les problèmes, pourtant je crois qu'on s'amusera mieux et nous aurons plus de liberté. On va sortir le soir et rentrer tard.

Nous irons à une station balnéaire qui s'appelle Langlois où les plages ne sont pas trop fréquentées et il y a un petit parc d'attractions. Nous allons aussi faire des excursions à un port de pêche dans la région et le soir, il y a beaucoup de boîtes de nuit. Nous n'avons pas encore réservé de chambres, mais je voudrais choisir un hôtel à prix raisonnable avec une salle de jeux où on peut s'amuser s'il fait mauvais.

Answer the questions **in English**.

Example: Where does Amadou usually go on holiday? ......the south-west of France......

(a) According to Amadou, what are the **two** disadvantages of going on holiday with friends?

(i) .... **(ii)** .... *(2 marks)*

(b) Why does Amadou think he will have a better time on holiday with friends? Give **two** reasons.

(i) .... **(ii)** .... *(2 marks)*

(c) What does Amadou say about the beaches in Langlois?

.... *(1 mark)*

(d) What can you do in the evening at Langlois?

.... *(1 mark)*

(e) What **two** things is Amadou looking for in his choice of hotel?

(i) .... **(ii)** .... *(2 marks)*

52 My next holiday

Listen to Paul talking about going on holiday to Morzine.

Choose the correct ending for each sentence from the grid. Write the correct letter in each box.

Example: Paul is going with [C]

(a) They will stay [   ] *(1 mark)* **(c)** In the afternoons, he will [   ] *(1 mark)*

(b) In the mornings, he will [   ] *(1 mark)* **(d)** In the evenings, he will [   ] *(1 mark)*

A	ski	E	swim
B	in a hotel	F	eat out
C	his whole family	G	eat in
D	climb	H	in a flat
I	take long walks		

- You will not be expected to know names of towns, but you must be able to recognise that the name of a town is not a word that might be part of an answer.

- Make sure you can recognise the names of major places like Paris – pronounced in the French way, of course!

Holiday experiences

53 The end of the holidays

Ouième is emailing her holiday experiences to her Welsh penfriend.

effacer répondre répondre à tous avant imprimer

Bonjour Angharad!

Malheureusement, les vacances sont finies pour moi! Dans l'ensemble, j'ai passé quinze jours très agréables à Menton. Il a fait chaud tous les jours, mais je n'ai pas pu nager dans la mer parce que l'eau était trop froide pour moi. Mais j'ai vu plusieurs petits qui semblaient contents de se baigner!

Tous les soirs, nous sommes allés à la ville de Nice parce qu'il y avait plus de choses à faire pour les personnes de notre âge. Et qu'est-ce qu'ils sont sympas, les gens de là-bas!

Amicalement,

Ouième

Which of these statements are correct? Write the letters of the **four** correct statements in the boxes below.

A	Ouième spent more than a fortnight in Menton.
B	The holiday experience was pleasant, overall.
C	On certain days, the weather wasn't warm.
D	Everyone found the seawater too cold to swim in.
E	Some children went swimming in the sea.
F	On just one occasion, they visited Nice.
G	Nice offered activities for people of Ouième's age.
H	Ouième was impressed by the friendly nature of the local people.

☐ *(1 mark)*   ☐ *(1 mark)*   ☐ *(1 mark)*   ☐ *(1 mark)*

54 A previous holiday

Listen to Lucie talking about a holiday.

Who does each statement refer to? Write **L** (Lucie), **J** (Juliette) or **L/J** (both Lucie and Juliette) in each box.

Example: Always used to spend holidays in south-east France   L

(a) Often spent holidays in Spain   ☐   *(1 mark)*

(b) Travelled by fast train   ☐   *(1 mark)*

(c) Spent a holiday in Bordeaux   ☐   *(1 mark)*

(d) Went to Bordeaux by car   ☐   *(1 mark)*

(e) Stayed in a three-star hotel   ☐   *(1 mark)*

(f) Went to museums with parents   ☐   *(1 mark)*

Countries

1 Moving to Switzerland

Read Nabila's account of moving to Switzerland. Choose a word from the grid to complete each sentence and write the correct letter in the box.

Example: L'année [E] , mon père a trouvé un emploi en Suisse.

(a) Mes parents ont [ ] à acheter une maison à Genève.   *(1 mark)*

(b) J'ai commencé à un nouveau [ ] près de chez nous.   *(1 mark)*

(c) D'abord, j'[ ] nerveuse, mais ça va mieux maintenant.   *(1 mark)*

(d) Il y a des élèves suisses et des élèves d'autres [ ] aussi.   *(1 mark)*

(e) Ma meilleure copine est [ ] .   *(1 mark)*

(f) Il y a [ ] de choses à faire à Genève et on ne s'ennuie jamais.   *(1 mark)*

(g) Hier, j'ai visité un vieux [ ] avec mes amis de classe.   *(1 mark)*

(h) Quand même j'[ ] vivre en France dans le futur.   *(1 mark)*

A	décidé	H	aimerais
B	plein	I	veux
C	français	J	réussi
D	belge	K	étais
E	dernière	L	était
F	collège	M	nationalités
G	piscine	N	château

> Take care to check whether the word in the gap should be singular or plural, masculine or feminine.

2 Friends and family abroad

Listen to Johann talking about where his friends and family live. Write the correct letter in each box.

A	Japan	E	USA
B	Portugal	F	Germany
C	Spain	G	Wales
D	Italy	H	England

Example: Paul [C]

1 Lily   [ ]   *(1 mark)*

2 Georges   [ ]   *(1 mark)*

3 Luc   [ ]   *(1 mark)*

4 Grandmother   [ ]   *(1 mark)*

5 Marie   [ ]   *(1 mark)*

My house

3 My new house

Read Farida's description of her new house.

> Mes parents ont acheté une nouvelle maison, située en ville près du cinéma. C'est pratique pour aller faire du shopping mais il y a trop de bruit le soir et la nuit.
>
> La salle à manger me plaît beaucoup parce qu'elle est grande et on peut y manger facilement, même quand il y a des invités. Pourtant, le salon est très petit et il n'y a pas beaucoup d'espace. Je trouve la cuisine très bien équipée et moderne et je vais y préparer beaucoup de repas délicieux. Par contre, je n'aime pas la salle de bains parce qu'elle est démodée.
>
> Le jardin est joli avec des fleurs fantastiques, cependant il n'y a pas de pelouse, ce qui m'énerve.

What is Farida's opinion of each of the following? Write **P** (positive), **N** (negative) or **P/N** (both positive and negative) in each box.

(a) Situation of the house ☐ *(1 mark)*   **(d)** The kitchen ☐ *(1 mark)*

(b) The dining room ☐ *(1 mark)*   **(e)** The bathroom ☐ *(1 mark)*

(c) The living room ☐ *(1 mark)*   **(f)** The garden ☐ *(1 mark)*

4 Where do they live?

Listen to these people saying where they live. Write the correct letter in each box.

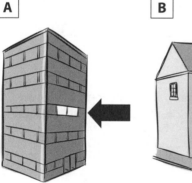

A   B   C   D

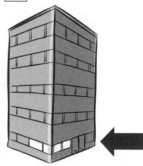

E   F   G   H

Example: F

1 ☐ *(1 mark)*   **3** ☐ *(1 mark)*

2 ☐ *(1 mark)*   **4** ☐ *(1 mark)*

My room

B

5 Léon's room

Read Léon's description of his room.

> Ma chambre me plaît beaucoup car c'est mon espace à moi. Je passe la plupart du temps sur mon ordinateur parce que j'adore tchater avec mes copains. Je partageais ma chambre avec mon frère, mais maintenant j'ai ma propre chambre car il est allé à l'université. C'est mieux car je peux me lever et me coucher quand je veux.
>
> Malheureusement, ma chambre est souvent en désordre et c'est ma mère qui la range toujours. Les rideaux sont bleus et les murs sont jaunes. Je viens d'acheter un tapis orange que j'adore et je voudrais avoir un nouveau fauteuil où je pourrais me détendre après avoir fini ma journée scolaire.

Read these statements. Write **T** (true), **F** (false) or **?** (not mentioned in the text) in each box.

Example: Léon likes his bedroom.   T

(a) Léon has a telephone in his room.   ☐   *(1 mark)*

(b) He shares a room with his brother.   ☐   *(1 mark)*

(c) He can get up and go to bed when he wants to.   ☐   *(1 mark)*

(d) He always tidies his room.   ☐   *(1 mark)*

(e) The curtains in his room are yellow.   ☐   *(1 mark)*

(f) There are posters on the wall.   ☐   *(1 mark)*

(g) He has bought an orange rug.   ☐   *(1 mark)*

(h) He would like a new armchair.   ☐   *(1 mark)*

> Be careful when distinguishing between 'false' and 'not mentioned in the text'. If something is not in the text, it doesn't mean that it is 'false' – it means that it is 'not mentioned in the text'.

C

6 Rémy's room

Listen to Rémy describing his bedroom. For each thing he mentions, give an advantage and a disadvantage **in English**.

Example:	Advantage	Disadvantage
Wardrobe	plenty of room for clothes	too big

	Advantage	Disadvantage
(i) Sharing his room		

(2 marks)

	Advantage	Disadvantage
(ii) Location of the room		

(2 marks)

Helping at home

7 What do they do to help?

What do these people do to help at home? Choose an activity from the grid to match each person. Write the correct letter in each box.

(a) Je garde mon petit frère de temps en temps. ☐   *(1 mark)*

(b) Je nettoie la cuisine le weekend. ☐   *(1 mark)*

(c) Je fais souvent du bricolage. ☐   *(1 mark)*

(d) Je dois laver la voiture de mon père. ☐   *(1 mark)*

(e) Je travaille dans le jardin en été. ☐   *(1 mark)*

(f) Je fais les courses pour une voisine. ☐   *(1 mark)*

(g) Je fais du babysitting pour ma tante. ☐   *(1 mark)*

(h) Je prépare le repas du soir tous les jours. ☐   *(1 mark)*

A	I look after my brother.	G	I wash the car.
B	I look after my sister.	H	I do DIY.
C	I go shopping.	I	I clean my bedroom.
D	I do the gardening.	J	I do babysitting.
E	I clean the kitchen.	K	I do the washing up.
F	I walk the dog.	L	I cook the evening meal.

8 Erica's household tasks

What is Erica's opinion of these household chores? Listen and write **P** (positive), **N** (negative) or **P/N** (both positive and negative) in each box.

Example: Cleaning the fridge | N |

1 Cooking dinner   ☐   *(1 mark)*

2 Tidying her room   ☐   *(1 mark)*

3 Babysitting   ☐   *(1 mark)*

4 Shopping for her grandmother   ☐   *(1 mark)*

5 Setting the table   ☐   *(1 mark)*

6 Walking the dog   ☐   *(1 mark)*

> When listening for opinions that are 'both positive and negative', words like *mais* (but), *pourtant* (however) and *cependant* (however) can sometimes give you a useful clue.

Where I live

9 My town

Read Hanif's description of his town.

> Je suis Hanif et je suis né au Cameroun. J'habite au dixième étage d'une HLM dans un quartier pauvre de Paris. Le bâtiment est en mauvais état et l'ascenseur ne marche pas depuis six mois. Notre appartement est beaucoup trop petit pour ma famille parce qu'on n'a que trois chambres mais j'ai trois sœurs et deux frères et mon père et ma mère.
>
> Il y a une usine tout près, ce qui veut dire qu'il y a souvent de la fumée dans l'atmosphère. À part les problèmes de pollution, c'est toujours bruyant et on risque d'être agressé si on sort après dix heures du soir. La semaine dernière, un de mes copains rentrait tard d'une fête quand un groupe de jeunes l'a pourchassé. Il a laissé tomber son portable qu'on a ramassé et il était vraiment triste de l'avoir perdu.
>
> À mon avis, on devrait construire un club des jeunes ou un centre de sport car il n'y a rien à faire ici pour les ados.

Answer these questions **in English**.

Example: Where was Hanif born? ....Cameroon.................

(a) Where in Paris does Hanif live? Give **two** details.

(i) ....   (ii) ....   *(2 marks)*

(b) Give **two** details about the building in which he lives.

(i) ....   (ii) ....   *(2 marks)*

(c) Why is the small size of the flat a problem?

....   *(1 mark)*

(d) Give any **two** problems about the area in which Hanif lives.

(i) ....   (ii) ....   *(2 marks)*

(e) What happened to his friend? Give **two** details.

(i) ....   (ii) ....   *(2 marks)*

(f) What does Hanif suggest would be an improvement to young people's lives in the area?

....   *(1 mark)*

10 My region

Listen to Caroline and Ludovic talking about where they live.

Which of these statements are true? Write the correct **four** letters in the boxes.

A	Caroline recently moved to France.	F	Ludovic is French.
B	She is now living with her father.	G	He has always lived in France.
C	She used to live in a tent.	H	He thinks that his town is an unsafe place.
D	She found it easy to make friends.	I	He thinks that his town lacks facilities.
E	She would like to live in a hot country in the future.	J	He would like to move to the countryside in the future.

☐ *(1 mark)*   ☐ *(1 mark)*   ☐ *(1 mark)*   ☐ *(1 mark)*

Places in town

11 A new shopping centre

You see this advertisement for a shopping centre.

Centre Commercial de la Falaise

Ce nouveau centre commercial vous propose:

▷ Cent-dix magasins
▷ Parking gratuit
▷ Cinq salles de cinéma
▷ Grand choix de restaurants et de cafés

▷ À trois kilomètres de l'autoroute A6
▷ Le centre commercial est non-fumeur.

Ouvert entre 10 heures et 19 heures du lundi au samedi
Fermé le dimanche

Answer the following questions **in English**. You do not need to answer in full sentences.

(a) How many shops are there? .... *(1 mark)*

(b) How far is the centre from the nearest motorway? .... *(1 mark)*

(c) What restriction is placed upon visitors? .... *(1 mark)*

(d) On which day or days is the centre closed? .... *(1 mark)*

> Remember to answer the questions **in English**.

12 The Caria Zoo

Listen to this advertisement for the Caria Zoo in France.

Choose the correct ending for each sentence. Write the correct letter in each box.

Example: The park is home to …

A	120 cats.
B	140 cats.
C	60 cats.

B

(a) In summer, the zoo opens at …

A	9.15 a.m.
B	9.30 a.m.
C	9.45 a.m.

(1 mark)

(b) The annual closure ends on …

A	27th February.
B	7th February.
C	17th February.

(1 mark)

(c) Children pay less if they are aged under …

A	nine.
B	twelve.
C	ten.

(1 mark)

(d) You may not take into the zoo …

A	your own dog.
B	food for the animals.
C	your mobile phone.

(1 mark)

Things to do in town

13 Holidays in Saint-Malo

Read Annie's email about Saint-Malo.

⊘ effacer   ↰ répondre   ↰ répondre à tous   → avant   🖨 imprimer

Tous les ans, ma famille et moi, nous passons une semaine de vacances dans la ville de Saint-Malo. En général, nous restons dans un hôtel qui est situé en face de la mer.

La plage est assez belle, mais je trouve que l'eau de mer est trop froide pour faire de la natation. Beaucoup de touristes britanniques visitent Saint-Malo.

Beaucoup de restaurants de Saint-Malo ont une bonne réputation! La plupart des touristes adorent dîner dans les nombreux restaurants qui servent du poisson et des fruits de mer.

En ville, ma mère préfère regarder dans les magasins de souvenirs, alors que mon père adore voir les beaux bateaux dans le vieux port. Personnellement, je n'aime pas le jour du marché car il y a trop de touristes!

Read these statements. Write **T** (true), **F** (false) or **?** (not mentioned in the text) in each box.

Example: Annie's family have never been to Saint-Malo. | F |

(a) Annie's family is large. ☐ *(1 mark)*

(b) They stay in a hotel opposite the sea. ☐ *(1 mark)*

(c) She finds the seawater warm in Saint-Malo. ☐ *(1 mark)*

(d) Lots of British tourists go to Saint-Malo. ☐ *(1 mark)*

(e) There are lots of fish restaurants there. ☐ *(1 mark)*

(f) Annie's dad is older than her mum. ☐ *(1 mark)*

(g) Annie thinks it's too crowded on market days. ☐ *(1 mark)*

14 A discussion about a town

Listen to Lysette and Cyrille discussing things to do in Cyrille's home town.

Which of these statements are correct? Write the correct **five** letters in the boxes.

A	The town hall was built in the 14th century.
B	Cyrille's mum thinks the town hall is a good place to visit.
C	Cyrille is not impressed by the church in his town.
D	Cyrille thinks the castle is impressive.
E	His dad likes the palace in the town.
F	His dad enjoys relaxing in his garden.
G	Lysette thinks the town is a special place.
H	Cyrille is well informed about future events in his town.
I	Lysette has just been to the tourist information office.
J	Lysette would like to go to the beach.
K	According to Cyrille, the weather will improve later in the day.

☐ *(1 mark)*   ☐ *(1 mark)*   ☐ *(1 mark)*   ☐ *(1 mark)*   ☐ *(1 mark)*

Tourist attractions

E *READING*

15 Tourism

Read these sentences about tourist attractions in a town.

Choose a place from the grid to go with each sentence. Write the correct letter in each box.

Example: On peut visiter la galerie d'art moderne en ville. $\boxed{G}$

(a)	On peut visiter un château qui date de 1232.	☐ *(1 mark)*
(b)	Les touristes peuvent aller dans les grands magasins.	☐ *(1 mark)*
(c)	Pour ceux qui aiment manger en ville, il y a beaucoup de choix.	☐ *(1 mark)*
(d)	Nous avons une église historique qui est populaire avec les touristes.	☐ *(1 mark)*
(e)	On peut y faire beaucoup de sports.	☐ *(1 mark)*
(f)	Si on est blessé, on peut y aller sans problèmes.	☐ *(1 mark)*
(g)	Les visiteurs peuvent s'informer ici.	☐ *(1 mark)*

A	disco	**G**	art gallery
B	department stores	**H**	bank
C	castle	**I**	church
D	leisure centre	**J**	police station
E	restaurants	**K**	shows
F	tourist office	**L**	hospital

> Try to build up banks of French words and phrases that mean the same as each other (for example *faire du vélo, faire du cyclisme*) or that are related to each other (for example *nager, natation, piscine*).

16 Activities in town

Listen to these people talking about what they like doing in town. Answer the questions **in English**.

Example: What does Corinne like doing? .... *going to the cinema* ....

1 What did Éric do last weekend?

.... *(1 mark)*

2 What is Servane planning to do next weekend?

.... *(1 mark)*

3 Where did Manon spend time this morning and why?

(a) .... **(b)** .... *(2 marks)*

4 What does Boris like doing most?

.... *(1 mark)*

Signs around town

17 Understanding signs

Read the following signs.

A

La banque est fermée le samedi matin.

B

Ouvert tous les jours sauf le dimanche.

C

Prenez le bus, c'est très confortable!

D

Interdit à tous les véhicules entre 9h et 18h, sauf services d'urgence.

E

Tarif réduit pour les moins de dix-huit ans

F

Le samedi, on reste ouvert jusqu'à midi.

G

La gare est ouverte tous les jours, même à Noël.

H

Trois heures de parking gratuit, tous les jours.

I

Parking gratuit toute la journée!

Which signs are these? Write the correct letter in each box.

Example: Discounts for people under 18 years old. `E`

(a) Restrictions on traffic.   ☐   *(1 mark)*

(b) Free parking all day.   ☐   *(1 mark)*

(c) Not open on Saturday mornings.   ☐   *(1 mark)*

(d) Open every day.   ☐   *(1 mark)*

18 Opening times

Listen to the information about opening times. At what time do these places open?

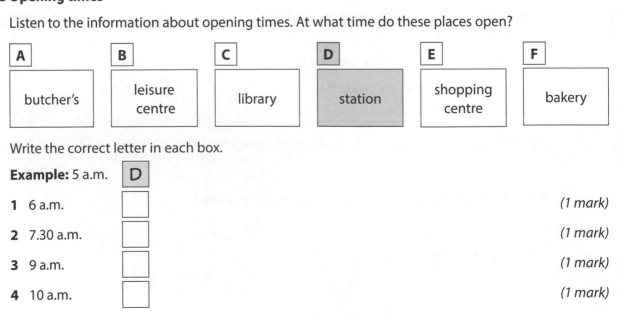

A	B	C	D	E	F
butcher's	leisure centre	library	station	shopping centre	bakery

Write the correct letter in each box.

Example: 5 a.m. `D`

1 6 a.m.   ☐   *(1 mark)*

2 7.30 a.m.   ☐   *(1 mark)*

3 9 a.m.   ☐   *(1 mark)*

4 10 a.m.   ☐   *(1 mark)*

Opinions of where you live

19 Where I live

Read what these young men say about their local area.

> **David:** Dans ma ville, il y a beaucoup de possibilités pour les personnes qui désirent pratiquer le sport. Par contre, il n'y a plus de cinéma. En hiver, il fait très froid, mais le beau temps arrive au mois de mai!

> **Luc:** Ça fait dix ans que j'habite par ici et je trouve qu'il ne fait jamais froid. Je n'aimerais pas quitter ma région parce que tous mes amis sont là. La seule difficulté pour moi, c'est qu'il n'y a pas beaucoup de facilités sportives.

> **Zachary:** Ma ville propose toutes sortes d'activités, comme les théâtres, les cinémas et les complexes sportifs. Malheureusement, je ne vais pas rester dans cette ville parce que je ne pourrai pas y trouver un bon travail.

Answer these questions. Write **D** (David), **L** (Luc) or **Z** (Zachary) in each box.

Example: Who has lived in the same area for ten years?   L

(a) Who has decided to leave the area where he lives?   ☐   *(1 mark)*

(b) Who lives in a town with few possibilities for sport?   ☐   *(1 mark)*

(c) Who never experiences cold weather where he lives?   ☐   *(1 mark)*

(d) Who lives in a town where there used to be a cinema?   ☐   *(1 mark)*

20 My town

Listen to these young people talking about their town. Which of these things do they mention? Are they advantages or disadvantages? Write the correct letters in the boxes.

A	traffic	F	factories
B	shopping	G	pollution
C	school	H	cinema
D	noise	I	quiet atmosphere
E	sports facilities	J	historic monuments

> Listen out for positive and negative opinions so that you will know when the advantages and disadvantages are being discussed.

	Advantage	Disadvantage	
Example:	B	G	
1			*(2 marks)*
2			*(2 marks)*
3			*(2 marks)*

Town description

21 Anya's town

Read Anya's account of her town.

> J'habite dans une petite ville qui s'appelle Chaumont, située dans le sud-est de la France, depuis dix-huit mois. Avant, j'habitais dans une banlieue de Lyon où je suis née. À vrai dire, je n'aimais pas Lyon parce qu'il y avait trop de monde et beaucoup d'usines et c'était assez sale. Pourtant Chaumont est pittoresque et assez calme. Il n'y a jamais d'embouteillages et les gens ici sont pour la plupart très sympa.
>
> En été, des touristes viennent faire des sports nautiques comme la voile au lac qui est à cinq minutes de ma maison en auto et il y a plein de distractions en ville. Pour ceux qui aiment la nature, on peut observer des oiseaux rares et des fleurs sauvages. En plus, on va bientôt faire construire une patinoire et l'année dernière un nouveau centre commercial a ouvert ses portes. Selon moi, c'est une ville agréable et j'aime vivre ici.

Answer these questions **in English**.

Example: Where is Chaumont? ....*in the south-east of France*....

(a) How long has Anya been living in Chaumont?

.... *(1 mark)*

(b) Why did she not like Lyon? Give **two** reasons.

(i) ....   **(ii)** .... *(2 marks)*

(c) What does she say about road traffic in Chaumont?

.... *(1 mark)*

(d) Why do tourists come to Chaumont in summer?

.... *(1 mark)*

(e) Why might nature lovers enjoy visiting Chaumont? Give **two** details.

(i) ....   **(ii)** .... *(2 marks)*

(f) What does Anya say is going to happen soon?

.... *(1 mark)*

22 Where people live

Where do these young people live? Listen and write the correct letter in each box.

A	a small town at the seaside	F	a large town on the coast
B	a large industrial town	G	a small town near Paris
C	a large town in the south of France	H	a small town in the east of France
D	a fishing port	I	a historic town
E	a small town in the west of France	J	a ski resort

Example: J

1 ☐   *(1 mark)*   3 ☐   *(1 mark)*

2 ☐   *(1 mark)*   4 ☐   *(1 mark)*

Weather

23 What is the weather like?

Look at these weather conditions.

A   B   C   D

E   F   G   H

Choose a weather picture to go with each sentence. Write the correct letter in each box.

Example: À Lille, il neige beaucoup! B

(a) Aujourd'hui, il pleuvra à Marseille! ☐ *(1 mark)*

(b) Dans les Alpes, il y aura un orage. ☐ *(1 mark)*

(c) À Metz, le vent va causer des problèmes. ☐ *(1 mark)*

(d) Qu'est-ce qu'il fait froid à Paris! ☐ *(1 mark)*

(e) À Reims, il y aura du brouillard. ☐ *(1 mark)*

24 Weather forecast

Listen to this weather report.

Choose a word from the box to label each area of the map.

sunny	windy	raining	cold	foggy	snowing

North

(d) .... *(1 mark)*

Paris

Example: ..cold...............................

East

(a) .... *(1 mark)*

South

(b) .... *(1 mark)*

West

(c) .... *(1 mark)*

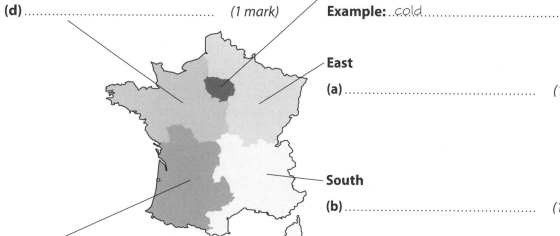

Celebrations at home

25 Birthdays

Read what three young people say about their birthdays.

> **Jamila**: Je viens d'avoir seize ans et pour mon anniversaire je suis allée en ville avec mes parents et nous avons dîné dans un restaurant chic. Après y avoir pris un repas délicieux, j'ai retrouvé quelques copines et nous avons continué la fête dans une boîte de nuit. Nous avons dansé jusqu'à minuit passé.

> **Karine**: Normalement, on organise une boum chez nous pour fêter mon anniversaire, mais l'année dernière mes parents ont décidé de louer une salle dans un hôtel et on y a invité des amis. Les plats étaient un peu trop épicés pour presque tout le monde, mais on s'est bien amusés à chanter et à bavarder ensemble.

> **Louise**: En général, je sors avec des copains pour célébrer mon anniversaire, mais cette année je vais rester chez moi. Ma famille a organisé un feu d'artifice et j'attends la soirée avec impatience. Nous allons aussi prendre un repas spécial sur la terrasse.

Answer the following questions. Write **J** (Jamila), **K** (Karine) or **L** (Louise) in each box.

Example: Who is 16?   ☐ J

(a) Who usually spends her birthday at home?   ☐   *(1 mark)*

(b) Who will have fireworks at her birthday celebration?   ☐   *(1 mark)*

(c) Who went to a nightclub on her birthday?   ☐   *(1 mark)*

(d) Who had a celebration that went on late?   ☐   *(1 mark)*

(e) Who had food that most of the guests did not enjoy?   ☐   *(1 mark)*

(f) Who enjoyed singing?   ☐   *(1 mark)*

26 Special occasions

Which special occasion is each of these people talking about? Listen and write the correct letter in each box.

A	Easter	E	Christmas Eve
B	Christmas Day	F	All Saints' Day
C	New Year's Eve	G	a birthday
D	a wedding	H	New Year's Day

Example: G

1 ☐   *(1 mark)*

2 ☐   *(1 mark)*

3 ☐   *(1 mark)*

4 ☐   *(1 mark)*

Directions

27 Getting to David's house

Read these directions to David's house.

> Salut Jeremy! Désolé, mais je ne pourrai pas venir te chercher à la gare. En sortant de la gare, ça te prendra une trentaine de minutes à pied.
>
> Alors, tu vas tourner à gauche quand tu quitteras la gare. Il y a une petite colline qui ne prend que cinq minutes à monter, mais ce sera plus facile demain soir quand tu seras sur le chemin du retour! N'oublie pas de tourner à droite en face de la station-service. Puis tu vas aller tout droit, jusqu'à la librairie. À ce moment-là, si tu regardes bien, tu verras notre magnifique mairie. Par contre, si tu passes directement devant un grand hôpital sur ta gauche, c'est que tu es allé trop loin!
>
> Fais très attention en traversant toutes les routes parce qu'il faut regarder d'abord à gauche, pas comme en Angleterre. Malheureusement, il n'y a que très peu de zones piétonnes chez nous.

> Be careful with the negative *ne … que*, which means 'only'.

Which of these statements are correct? Write the correct **four** letters in the boxes.

A	David lives about 30 minutes walk from the station.
B	There is a short hill to walk down.
C	Part of the route is uphill.
D	Turn right opposite a petrol station.
E	There is a library along this route.
F	At one point, the town hall is visible.
G	The route passes in front of a hospital.
H	Jeremy offers road safety advice to David.

Example: A

☐ *(1 mark)*   ☐ *(1 mark)*   ☐ *(1 mark)*   ☐ *(1 mark)*

28 Getting home

Listen. How do these teenagers get home? Write the correct letter in each box.

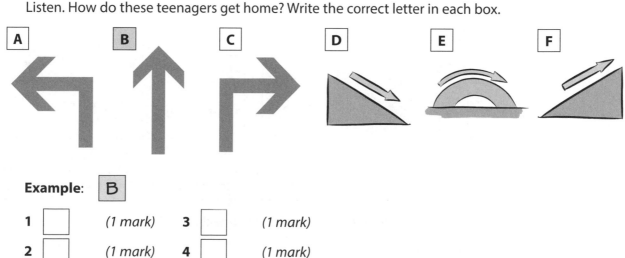

Example: B

1 ☐ *(1 mark)*   3 ☐ *(1 mark)*

2 ☐ *(1 mark)*   4 ☐ *(1 mark)*

At the railway station

29 Signs at the railway station

Read these signs.

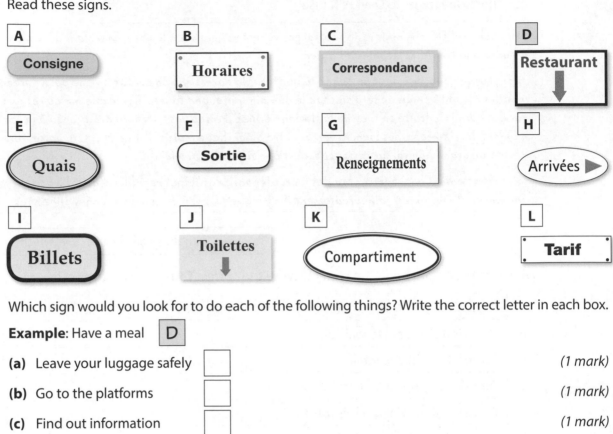

A	Consigne
B	Horaires
C	Correspondance
D	Restaurant ↓
E	Quais
F	Sortie
G	Renseignements
H	Arrivées ▶
I	Billets
J	Toilettes ↓
K	Compartiment
L	Tarif

Which sign would you look for to do each of the following things? Write the correct letter in each box.

Example: Have a meal   D

(a) Leave your luggage safely ☐ *(1 mark)*

(b) Go to the platforms ☐ *(1 mark)*

(c) Find out information ☐ *(1 mark)*

(d) Leave the station ☐ *(1 mark)*

(e) Buy tickets ☐ *(1 mark)*

(f) Change trains ☐ *(1 mark)*

(g) Check a timetable ☐ *(1 mark)*

(h) Go to the toilet ☐ *(1 mark)*

30 A class outing

The class is waiting at the railway station.

A	B	C	D	E	F
café	toilet	sitting on suitcase	telephone	magazine kiosk	waiting room

> Make good use of reading time before you listen. Look at A–F and try to work out what French words you might hear.

Where has each person gone? Listen and write the correct letter in each box.

Example: Thomas   B

1 Daniella ☐ *(1 mark)*   3 Raphaël ☐ *(1 mark)*

2 Noah ☐ *(1 mark)*   4 Nanette ☐ *(1 mark)*

Travelling

READING

31 How do they travel?

 **A**
 **B**
 **C**
 **D**

 **E**
 **F**
 **G**
 **H**

What type of transport does each person mention? Write the correct letter in each box.

Example: Je vais prendre le train.   **B**

(a) Je vais au collège à vélo.   ☐   *(1 mark)*

(b) En général, je voyage à moto.   ☐   *(1 mark)*

(c) L'avion, c'est pour les longs voyages.   ☐   *(1 mark)*

(d) Prendre ma voiture, c'est très pratique.   ☐   *(1 mark)*

LISTENING 61

32 Travelling around town

Marianne is talking about how she travels.

 **A**
 **B**
 **C**

 **D**
 **E**
 **F**

How does she get to these places? Listen and write the correct letter in each box.

Example: School   **D**

(a) Gym   ☐   *(1 mark)*   **(c)** Swimming pool   ☐   *(1 mark)*

(b) Museum   ☐   *(1 mark)*   **(d)** Church   ☐   *(1 mark)*

Transport

33 A transport blog

Read the following blog entries from a discussion about holiday transport.

Blog Vacances! Donnez votre opinion!

David: En vacances, j'ai bien aimé prendre les transports en commun.

Clara: Pour moi, voyager, ça doit représenter une aventure.

Manon: J'ai pris la décision de prendre ma propre voiture.

Antoine: Malheureusement, le bus ne passe pas devant l'hôtel.

Tamsir: Attendre aux arrêts d'autobus, c'est ennuyeux.

Laure: Pour visiter la région, je vais prendre une voiture de location.

Béatrice: Ça ne me dérange jamais de conduire pendant les vacances.

Oscar: En général, l'idée de conduire en vacances ne me plaît pas.

Hugo: Prendre les transports en commun, ce n'est pas un plaisir pour moi.

Who says the following? Write the correct name beside each sentence.

Example: Travelling should be an adventure. .... Clara

(a) I don't like driving on holiday. .... *(1 mark)*

(b) I don't like spending time waiting for public transport. .... *(1 mark)*

(c) I'm not keen on public transport. .... *(1 mark)*

(d) I am going to hire a car. .... *(1 mark)*

34 Trams in France

Listen to the report about trams in France.

Answer the following questions **in English**.

> Keep your answers as short as possible, but make sure you give all the required information. One word and one number will answer question (a).

(i) **(a)** When were trams at the height of their success in France?

.... *(1 mark)*

(b) What **two** things encouraged the popularity of the motor car?

.... *(2 marks)*

(c) What effect did this have on trams?

.... *(1 mark)*

(ii) **(a)** After 1973, what **two** things encouraged new investment in trams?

.... *(2 marks)*

(b) How is urban space better used nowadays?

.... *(1 mark)*

(c) How many French towns now have a tram network?

.... *(1 mark)*

The environment

35 Environmental issues

Read about these issues affecting the environment.

Choose a word from the grid to fill the gap in each sentence. Write the correct letter in each box.

Example: La pollution est un problème ☐ B

(a) On est en train de ☐ la planète. *(1 mark)*

(b) À mon avis, il ☐ essayer de protéger la terre. *(1 mark)*

(c) Un problème ☐ , c'est le déboisement. *(1 mark)*

(d) Beaucoup d' ☐ sont menacés par les actions de l'homme. *(1 mark)*

(e) Certains pensent que la pollution est causée par les ☐ *(1 mark)*

(f) Le niveau de la ☐ monte et beaucoup d'îles sont en danger de disparition. *(1 mark)*

(g) L' ☐ de serre provoque le réchauffement de la terre. *(1 mark)*

(h) Les ☐ ne sont pas d'accord quand on discute la cause des
problèmes de l'environnement. *(1 mark)*

A	scientifiques	G	détruire
B	mondial	H	aller
C	vagues	I	animaux
D	usines	J	mer
E	voudrais	K	grave
F	faut	L	effet

36 World problems

Listen to this discussion about world problems. Which of the statements below are true? Write the correct **four** letters in the boxes.

A	Monsieur Dumas does not think that pollution is one of the most serious problems.
B	He says that temperatures are reaching record highs every year.
C	According to Monsieur Dumas, global warming causes floods.
D	Monsieur Dumas thinks the situation is getting slightly easier.
E	He blames the big industrialised countries for making the situation worse.
F	Monsieur Dumas has just returned from a trip to China.
G	He says that people should reduce the amount of air travel they do.
I	He says that we are using less electricity nowadays.

☐ *(1 mark)* ☐ *(1 mark)* ☐ *(1 mark)* ☐ *(1 mark)*

Environmental problems

37 Problems in Rouen

Read this account by Sophie about the main problems in the town where she lives. Write **T** (true), **F** (false) or **?** (not mentioned in the text) next to each statement.

> Depuis ma naissance, j'habite à Rouen dans le nord de la France. Les problèmes dans ma ville sont assez graves. Les transports en commun sont nuls car les bus ne sont pas fréquents et les billets de train sont trop chers. La circulation est donc devenue un gros problème, surtout aux heures d'affluence. Nous n'avons pas assez de pistes cyclables, donc beaucoup de gens doivent voyager en voiture.
>
> Les rues ne sont pas propres et on voit partout des déchets par terre, ce qui me rend vraiment furieuse. On vient d'installer des poubelles supplémentaires dans les rues et maintenant on en a assez, mais des gens ont continué à jeter des déchets sur les trottoirs.
>
> *Sophie*

Example: Sophie lives in Rouen.   `T`

(a) Sophie has always lived in Rouen.   ☐   *(1 mark)*

(b) The trams run every 30 minutes in Rouen.   ☐   *(1 mark)*

(c) Train tickets are not too dear.   ☐   *(1 mark)*

(d) Traffic problems exist in the town.   ☐   *(1 mark)*

(e) There are enough cycle paths in Rouen.   ☐   *(1 mark)*

(f) People don't use their cars much in Rouen.   ☐   *(1 mark)*

(g) More rubbish bins have been placed in the streets.   ☐   *(1 mark)*

(h) It costs a lot to sort out the rubbish problem.   ☐   *(1 mark)*

38 Town problems

Listen to these people talking about issues in a town. Write the correct letter in each box.

A	recycling glass	E	recycling paper
B	recycling plastic	F	litter in the streets
C	pedestrian zones	G	public transport
D	noise	H	smoke

Example: `B`

1 ☐   *(1 mark)*   **3** ☐   *(1 mark)*

2 ☐   *(1 mark)*   **4** ☐   *(1 mark)*

What I do to be 'green'

C READING

39 Helping the environment

Read about what these three young people do to help the environment.

> **Denis**: Je fais beaucoup pour l'environnement, par exemple j'achète des produits bio si possible et j'utilise des sacs en plastique plusieurs fois au supermarché. Je vais partout en ville en vélo mais je sais que je devrais recycler plus de carton.

> **Maurice**: J'essaie de conserver de l'eau. Je prends une douche au lieu d'un bain et je me brosse les dents, le robinet fermé. À l'avenir, je vais dire à mes parents de baisser le chauffage central aussi.

> **Yannick**: Pour conserver de l'énergie, j'essaie de toujours éteindre toutes les lumières chez moi quand je sors d'une pièce. Hier, j'ai refusé un sac en plastique dans un magasin et je vais recycler toutes les articles en verre au lieu de les jeter dans la poubelle.

> Remember to look beyond the obvious word. For example, *conserver* (to save) appears in two of the texts so you will need to look at what follows it in order to work out the correct answers.

Which person best fits each statement? Write **D** (Denis), **M** (Maurice) or **Y** (Yannick) in each box.

Example: I buy green products. | D |

(a) I save water.   ☐   *(1 mark)*

(b) I recently did not use a plastic bag.   ☐   *(1 mark)*

(c) I try to use a greener way to get around.   ☐   *(1 mark)*

(d) I am going to suggest changing the heating arrangements.   ☐   *(1 mark)*

(e) I know that I should recycle cardboard.   ☐   *(1 mark)*

(f) I already try to save energy by making sure lights are turned off.   ☐   *(1 mark)*

E LISTENING 65

40 Green solutions

What does each person do to be green? Listen and choose a picture to match each speaker. Write the correct letter in each box.

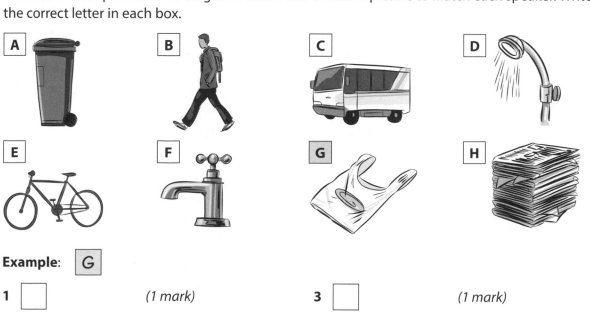

Example: | G |

1 ☐   *(1 mark)*   3 ☐   *(1 mark)*

2 ☐   *(1 mark)*   4 ☐   *(1 mark)*

News headlines

41 World news

Read these headlines.

A	Earthquake causes problems for locals
B	War in Africa
C	Floods cause chaos
D	Adverse weather causes havoc
E	Overpopulation an even bigger issue
F	Fire damages many buildings in town
G	Animals face extinction
H	Deforestation on the increase
I	Peace agreed in local dispute

Choose a headline from above to match each news item. Write the correct letter in each box.

Example: Le déboisement devient un problème de plus en plus sérieux. H

(a) Dans les pays surpeuplés, les risques de faim sont très graves. Il faut assurer qu'on a assez à manger. ☐ *(1 mark)*

(b) Un tremblement de terre a détruit beaucoup de bâtiments dans la petite ville de Sarsa en Algérie. ☐ *(1 mark)*

(c) Des vents extrêmement forts ont provoqué des dégâts graves sur une île dans l'océan Atlantique. ☐ *(1 mark)*

(d) La ville de Mariatna a été inondée hier. Beaucoup d'habitants ont quitté leur maison sans pouvoir prendre toutes leurs affaires et la pluie continue à tomber. ☐ *(1 mark)*

42 Radio headlines

Listen to the headlines on the radio.

Choose the correct ending for each sentence. Write the correct letter in each box.

1 The music festival is in …

A	Spain.
B	Portugal.
C	Germany.

☐ *(1 mark)*

2 The number of cars involved in the accident is …

A	about 10.
B	about 20.
C	about 100.

☐ *(1 mark)*

3 The problem mentioned is …

A	at the station.
B	at the town hall.
C	at the tourist office.

☐ *(1 mark)*

4 The shop will reopen …

A	on Friday.
B	on Thursday.
C	on Saturday.

☐ *(1 mark)*

School subjects

1 School subjects

A   B   C 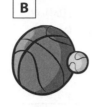 D   E

F  G  H  I

Which subject is being discussed? Write the correct letter in each box.

Example: Mon professeur de maths est très sympa. ☐ D

(a) J'aime bien l'histoire. ☐ *(1 mark)*

(b) Ma matière favorite est l'éducation physique. ☐ *(1 mark)*

(c) Mon amie préfère l'informatique. ☐ *(1 mark)*

(d) Le dessin, c'est super! ☐ *(1 mark)*

2 My lessons

Listen to Lucas talking about his lessons at school.

Decide which **five** of these statements are true. Write the correct letters in the boxes.

A	Lucas loves maths.
B	Lucas has changed his opinion about maths.
C	He doesn't mind German.
D	He has two hours of German a week.
E	He has fewer periods of chemistry than German each week.
F	He finds chemistry interesting.
G	He likes his chemistry teacher.
H	He doesn't mind Spanish.
I	He does gymnastics three times a week.
J	His favourite subject is PE.

Try to listen to everything relating to each statement before you make your decision – there might be some extra information that makes you change your mind

☐ *(1 mark)* ☐ *(1 mark)* ☐ *(1 mark)* ☐ *(1 mark)* ☐ *(1 mark)*

Opinions of school

3 My school

> - Remember that this sort of activity tests your grammar! For example, *les* in sentence (d) must be followed by a plural word, which would normally end in *-s* or sometimes *-x*.
> - Activities like this often test your knowledge of time frames, too. Remember that words like *prochain* (next) and *demain* (tomorrow) refer to future events, whereas *dernier* (last) and *hier* (yesterday) refer to the past.

Choose a word from the grid to fill each gap. Write the correct letter in each box.

Example: J'ai trop de ☐C le soir.

(a) J'ai peur d'☐ en maths. *(1 mark)*

(b) Dans mon école, il y a plus de ☐ étudiants. *(1 mark)*

(c) Ma copine Sarah est très ☐ en dessin. *(1 mark)*

(d) Ma matière préférée, c'est les ☐ vivantes. *(1 mark)*

(e) Je m'entends bien avec mon ☐, qui s'appelle Monsieur Laclos. *(1 mark)*

(f) J'ai ☐ de bonnes notes en musique. *(1 mark)*

(g) Je trouve l'anglais très ☐. *(1 mark)*

(h) Je vais passer un examen de français ☐. *(1 mark)*

A	réussir	F	facile	K	maths
B	hier	G	fort	L	échouer
C	devoirs	H	copine	M	élèves
D	langues	I	directeur	N	mille
E	forte	J	toujours	O	demain

4 Muriel's school

Listen to Muriel talking about her school. What does she think of each of the following? Write **P** (positive), **N** (negative) or **P/N** (both positive and negative) in each box.

Example: The buildings   P/N

1 The school day   ☐   *(1 mark)*

2 The canteen   ☐   *(1 mark)*

3 The teachers   ☐   *(1 mark)*

4 Homework   ☐   *(1 mark)*

5 Sports and after-school clubs   ☐   *(1 mark)*

6 French   ☐   *(1 mark)*

School routine

5 School life

Read each person's description of their school day.

> **Jean:** Au collège, on commence à huit heures et à mon avis la journée est trop longue car on a sept cours d'une heure par jour. Je fais des progrès en dessin et en maths mais je suis faible en anglais. Le soir, je n'ai pas de temps pour m'amuser parce que je dois faire mes devoirs!

> **Marcus:** Ma journée commence tôt car je dois prendre le car de ramassage pour arriver au collège avant huit heures quand les cours commencent. Après deux cours, on a une récréation qui dure dix minutes mais on a encore deux cours avant la pause-déjeuner. Chaque cours dure cinquante minutes. Moi, j'attends les grandes vacances avec impatience.

> **Thibault:** Je vais au collège en voiture avec mon père qui est prof à mon école. Je ne fais pas de progrès en maths, ce qui m'énerve car je travaille bien en classe mais je ne comprends pas mon professeur qui n'explique pas bien les choses. La journée n'est pas trop longue parce qu'on finit à trois heures de l'après-midi.

Which person best fits each statement below? Write **J** (Jean), **M** (Marcus) or **T** (Thibault) in each box.

Example: There are seven lessons per day.   ☐ J

(a) I go to school by car.   ☐   *(1 mark)*

(b) I'm making progress in maths.   ☐   *(1 mark)*

(c) I cannot wait for the summer.   ☐   *(1 mark)*

(d) My school day is too long.   ☐   *(1 mark)*

(e) My teacher is stopping me from doing better.   ☐   *(1 mark)*

(f) Each lesson is under an hour long.   ☐   *(1 mark)*

6 My school day

Listen to these young people talking about their school routine. Answer the questions **in English**.

Example: When does school start for Jean-Claude? ....*8.30*..................

1 When does school end for Pauline? ....   *(1 mark)*

2 What does Sophie do during break? ....   *(1 mark)*

3 How long is each lesson in Thomas's school? ....   *(1 mark)*

4 Where does Annie meet her friend? ....   *(1 mark)*

Comparing schools

7   French and English schools

Read Marie's comparison of schools in Paris and London.

> Ici en France, ma semaine au collège commence à huit heures le lundi matin. En général, les cours durent une heure, mais c'est souvent plus court en Angleterre. Moi, je rentre chez moi à l'heure du déjeuner. Mes cours finissent assez tard l'après-midi, sauf le vendredi. En France, nous avons cours le samedi matin. Quelle horreur!
>
> Mon correspondant anglais s'appelle Danny. Il est content d'être élève en Angleterre, mais il aime bien visiter la France. Il n'aime pas la couleur de l'uniforme qu'il porte, mais il dit que c'est confortable. Danny étudie la religion, mais ce n'est pas sa matière préférée. Il pense que les professeurs sont plus sévères en France qu'en Angleterre.

> Where two or more people are mentioned in a text, make sure that your answers relate to the correct person.

Which of these issues are mentioned in the text? Write the correct **four** letters in the boxes.

A	School starting time in France	**F**	Danny's liking of school in the UK
B	Identical length of lessons in both cities	**G**	Marie's opinions on school uniform
C	Going home for lunch	**H**	Danny's favourite subject
D	Very late finish to lessons on Fridays	**I**	Teachers being less strict in England
E	Dislike of Saturday morning lessons		

Example: A

☐ *(1 mark)*   ☐ *(1 mark)*   ☐ *(1 mark)*   ☐ *(1 mark)*

8   An English school

Listen to Rhéa telling her mum about her day in an English school.

Decide which of these statements are true. Write the correct **four** letters in the boxes.

A	The English school starts at 8.45 a.m.
B	School starts earlier in the English school than in France.
C	Rhéa has met the principal of the school.
D	The school day is shorter in England.
E	Rhéa must stay in school all day in France.
F	In France, Rhéa has a coffee at break time.
G	There are three lessons in the afternoon in the English school.
H	Lots of pupils stay behind after lessons in the English school.
I	Rhéa has been to a nursery school with her penfriend.

☐ *(1 mark)*   ☐ *(1 mark)*   ☐ *(1 mark)*   ☐ *(1 mark)*

Primary school

9 Memories of primary school

Read these memories of primary school.

A	Chaque cours durait trois quarts d'heure.
B	On jouait dans la cour pendant la récréation.
C	Nous y arrivions à huit heures du matin.
D	Dans la cour de récréation, pas trop de règles à suivre!
E	L'institutrice pensait qu'il était important d'être polie envers tous ses élèves.
F	Il était interdit de jouer pendant les cours.
G	La récréation ne durait que dix minutes.
H	Notre institutrice nous demandait d'être toujours polis.
I	Le dernier cours se terminait à quatre heures.
J	J'allais à l'école à pied. Le voyage ne durait que quinze minutes.
K	On chantait tous les jours en classe.

Choose a memory from above to match each of the following. Write the correct letter in each box.

Example: The time pupils arrived at school   [C]

(a) Teacher showing courtesy towards pupils   [ ]   *(1 mark)*

(b) Length of each lesson   [ ]   *(1 mark)*

(c) What pupils did during breaks   [ ]   *(1 mark)*

(d) Rule applied during lessons   [ ]   *(1 mark)*

(e) Daily classroom activity   [ ]   *(1 mark)*

> Be careful with French words that look similar to English words. For example, *un cours* is a lesson, but *la cour* is the playground or school yard!

10 Marine's primary school

Listen to Marine talking about her primary school.

Complete each sentence by writing the correct letter in the box.

1 She used to go to school …

A	on foot.
B	by car.
C	by bus.

[ ]   *(1 mark)*

2 They didn't have …

A	interactive whiteboards.
B	computers.
C	enough textbooks.

[ ]   *(1 mark)*

3 Every day, they used to …

A	play football.
B	read.
C	draw.

[ ]   *(1 mark)*

4 She thought her classroom was …

A	very big.
B	not big enough.
C	very pretty.

[ ]   *(1 mark)*

Rules at school

11 What must you do?

Read these classroom instructions and school rules.

A Arrivez avant huit heures.

B Apportez un stylo.

C Rangez vos livres.

D Faites attention au professeur.

E Pas de téléphones portables.

F Regardez le tableau blanc.

G Ne fumez pas.

H Faites les devoirs.

I Ne mangez pas en classe.

Which of the following rules are mentioned above? Write the correct letter in each box.

Example: Listen to the teacher. ☐ D

(a) No mobile phones. ☐ *(1 mark)*   **(d)** No eating in class. ☐ *(1 mark)*

(b) Arrive by eight o'clock. ☐ *(1 mark)*   **(e)** Bring a pen. ☐ *(1 mark)*

(c) Look at the whiteboard. ☐ *(1 mark)*

A/A* LISTENING 72

12 School rules

Listen to Annette talking about the rules in her school. Answer the questions **in English**.

> Remember there is no need to answer questions using a full sentence. However, you must ensure that you answer the questions as fully as you can, giving the information and details that you are asked for.

Part 1

1 What must students do before entering the classroom?

.... *(1 mark)*

2 What happened to Annette when she made an error?

.... *(1 mark)*

3 Under what circumstances does Annette agree with the rule about earrings?

.... *(1 mark)*

Part 2

4 What does Annette think is dangerous? .... *(1 mark)*

5 Which rule does she think is ridiculous? .... *(1 mark)*

6 Give **one** reason why she thinks this. .... *(1 mark)*

7 Which rule does she talk about last and what does she think of this rule?

   (a) .... **(b)** .... *(2 marks)*

Problems at school

C

READING

13 What problems do they have?

Read what five young people say about problems at school. Choose a problem from the grid to explain what each person is worried about and write the correct letter in each box.

(a) Je n'ai pas de confiance en moi en classe et je ne parle jamais aux professeurs. ☐ *(1 mark)*

(b) Mon souci principal au collège, c'est que je n'ai pas beaucoup de copains. Je suis très timide et silencieux. ☐ *(1 mark)*

(c) J'ai trop de travail scolaire. Je vais bientôt passer mes examens et je m'inquiète beaucoup. En plus, je ne peux pas discuter mes problèmes avec mes parents. ☐ *(1 mark)*

(d) Quand mes parents me demandent si j'ai des ennuis au collège, je suis obligé de mentir. J'ai de mauvaises notes dans la plupart de mes matières. ☐ *(1 mark)*

(e) Je ne peux pas réviser chez moi car mon petit frère fait trop de bruit. ☐ *(1 mark)*

> Remember that in activities like this there may be two or even more clues in each sentence so it may not matter if you cannot understand the whole sentence. Just one word or phrase could help you find the correct answer!

A	Being bullied in class	F	People being rude
B	Too much noise at home	G	Telling lies about academic success
C	Getting too many detentions	H	Losing friends
D	Don't have friends	I	Too much schoolwork
E	No confidence in lessons	J	Smoking at school

D

LISTENING

73

14 Problems and solutions

Listen to the advice given to young people who are having problems at school.

What should each person do to help solve the problem? Write the answers **in English** in the grid.

> When you are asked to answer in English:
> - be careful not to use any French words
> - make sure you give as much information as is needed to answer the question.

Example: Marc	Make more effort in maths	
1 Mohammed		*(1 mark)*
2 Luc		*(1 mark)*
3 Shana		*(1 mark)*
4 Mollie		*(1 mark)*
5 Claudine		*(1 mark)*

Future education

15 Élodie's plans

Read about Élodie's education plans.

> J'ai l'intention de quitter l'école à l'âge de dix-huit ans. En ce moment, j'étudie plus de dix matières au lycée, mais au mois d'octobre, je vais commencer mes études à l'université, si je réussis à avoir le diplôme nécessaire. Au mois de juin, je vais passer un examen qui s'appelle le baccalauréat. Ça va me demander beaucoup de temps!
>
> La plupart de mes amis ont décidé de chercher un emploi car ils ne veulent pas entrer à l'université. Et moi, si je veux avoir assez d'argent à l'université, je serai obligée de travailler à temps partiel. Mes parents sont médecins alors ils sont bien payés et ils pourraient me donner de l'argent tous les mois.

Read these statements. Write **T** (true), **F** (false) or **?** (not mentioned in the text) in each box.

Example: Élodie plans to leave school aged sixteen.　F

(a) She currently studies ten subjects.　☐　*(1 mark)*

(b) She enjoys studying.　☐　*(1 mark)*

(c) She has recently done her A levels.　☐　*(1 mark)*

(d) She will need a part-time job.　☐　*(1 mark)*

(e) Her parents cannot help her out financially.　☐　*(1 mark)*

(f) She would like to be a doctor.　☐　*(1 mark)*

16 Amina's plans

Listen to Amina talking about her future plans. Which **four** of the following statements are true? Write the correct letters in the boxes.

A	I'm doing my GCSEs this July.
B	I want to go to the local sixth form.
C	German is not my best subject.
D	I like talking to foreigners.
E	I've had to repeat Year 11.
F	I'm going to relax in the summer holidays.
G	I'm going to do a course in Spain.
H	I want to be a language teacher.
I	I don't want to go to university.

> Sometimes a verb will indicate the future because of its meaning and not because it is in the future tense – think of *espérer* and *devenir*!

☐ *(1 mark)*　☐ *(1 mark)*　☐ *(1 mark)*　☐ *(1 mark)*

Future plans

17 What are their plans?

Here are some future plans written by young French people. Choose a word from the grid to fill each gap. Write the correct letter in each box.

Example: Je ne ☐D☐ pas ce que je vais faire l'année prochaine.

(a) Après ☐ quitté le collège, je chercherai un emploi.

(b) Je ☐ partout dans le monde.

(c) Je voudrais avoir ma ☐ entreprise.

(d) J'espère ☐ un apprentissage.

(e) J'irai à l'université où j'☐ les maths.

(f) Si je trouve un bon emploi bien ☐, je serai riche.

(g) À l'université, je ferai une ☐ d'anglais.

(h) Je voudrais me ☐ un jour.

> Remember that after an apostrophe, the next word must start with a vowel or letter *h* in French – as in sentence (e). In an exam, try not to feel stressed or you might miss something obvious like this!

A	marier	H	avoir
B	licence	I	être
C	travail	J	voyagerai
D	sais	K	faire
E	étudierai	L	payé
F	aller	M	argent
G	étudiera	N	propre

18 My ideal job

Listen to these young people speaking about their ideal jobs.

What do they want to do? Write the correct letter in each box.

A	Lorry driver	D	Nurse	G	Engineer
B	Farmer	E	Teacher	H	Dentist
C	Chef	F	Shop manager	I	Doctor

Example: Paul ☐E☐

1 Janine ☐ *(1 mark)*

2 Marc ☐ *(1 mark)*

3 Marianne ☐ *(1 mark)*

4 Jacques ☐ *(1 mark)*

5 Louise ☐ *(1 mark)*

6 Céline ☐ *(1 mark)*

Had a go ☐   Nearly there ☐   Nailed it! ☐

Jobs

F READING

19 What do they do?

Look at these jobs.

A

B

C

D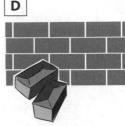

E

F

G

H

Which jobs do these people do? Write the correct letter in each box.

Example: Je travaille dans un hôpital.   **B**

(a) Ma mère répare des voitures.   ☐   *(1 mark)*

(b) Mes frères travaillent avec les animaux.   ☐   *(1 mark)*

(c) Son cousin travaille dans un magasin.   ☐   *(1 mark)*

(d) Yvette travaille dans un bureau en ville.   ☐   *(1 mark)*

D LISTENING **76**

20 A working family

Listen to Mireille talking about her family's jobs. Fill in the gaps **in English**.

Example: Mireille hopes to work as ...*an air hostess*...

1 Her dad is ....   *(1 mark)*

2 Her brother is ....   *(1 mark)*

3 Her sister is ....   *(1 mark)*

4 Her mum is ....   *(1 mark)*

5 Her cousin is ....   *(1 mark)*

6 Her best friend would like to become ....   *(1 mark)*

Job adverts

21 Job details

Read these job adverts.

> Travail à plein temps dans un restaurant, ouvert tous les jours sauf le dimanche.
>
> Salaire 15 euros par heure.

> Travail de bureau au centre-ville.
> Salaire à négocier.
> Lundi–vendredi de 8h à 16h.

> On cherche quelqu'un pour nettoyer la piscine au centre de sport.
> Weekends de 10h à 18h.
> Salaire 10 euros par heure.

> Propriétaire d'un petit magasin cherche vendeur.
> Mardi–vendredi de 9h à 18h.
> Réductions sur articles achetés de 10 pour cent.

Which **four** of these statements are true? Write the correct letters in the boxes.

A	The sports centre is looking for someone to clean the pool.
B	There are no full-time jobs being advertised.
C	The shop owner is looking for a salesperson.
D	There is a discount for workers at the restaurant.
E	The office work pays 15 euros per hour.
F	The office is in the town centre.
G	The restaurant is not open on Sundays.
H	The job in the shop is for five days a week.

☐ *(1 mark)*   ☐ *(1 mark)*   ☐ *(1 mark)*   ☐ *(1 mark)*

> Remember that the text of Higher questions is not always longer than that of Foundation questions. This announcement is short so you need to listen to every detail!

22 A radio announcement

Listen to this radio announcement.

Complete each sentence by writing the correct letter in the box.

1 The government will pay you a monthly sum of …

A	50 euros.
B	150 euros.
C	500 euros.

☐ *(1 mark)*

2 You will receive this money only if you …

A	work for a year.
B	do not work for a year.
C	do training for a year.

☐ *(1 mark)*

3 The announcement suggests you could …

A	work as a volunteer.
B	benefit from working part-time.
C	work for the local council.

☐ *(1 mark)*

4 You can get more information from …

A	the town hall.
B	the local library.
C	any local charitable organisation.

☐ *(1 mark)*

CV

23 My good points

Read these extracts from a CV.

> • Permis de conduire depuis 2009
> • Expérience du travail en équipe
> • Bon niveau en allemand
> • Intéressé par tous les sports, sauf le rugby et le tennis.
> • Expérience comme caissier
> • Libre à partir du mois prochain
> • Prêt à travailler dur
> • Pas d'absence maladie depuis quatre ans
> • Bon contact avec les collègues

Which of these statements are mentioned in the CV? Write the correct **five** letters in the boxes.

A	Good level in Spanish
B	Good attendance record
C	Experience of leading a team of workers
D	Willing to travel
E	Checkout experience
F	Experience of working abroad
G	Available from next month
H	Interested in most sports
I	Held driving licence since 2009

☐ *(1 mark)*   ☐ *(1 mark)*   ☐ *(1 mark)*   ☐ *(1 mark)*   ☐ *(1 mark)*

24 Paul's details

Listen to Paul talking about himself. Complete his details **in English**.

Example: Surname	Poirot	
Age		*(1 mark)*
Favourite school subject		*(1 mark)*
Favourite sport		*(1 mark)*
Hobby		*(1 mark)*

Job application

25 A letter of application

Read Sophie's letter of application.

Madame / Monsieur,

J'ai lu votre annonce sur Internet et je voudrais poser ma candidature pour le poste de secrétaire à votre école maternelle. Je travaille dans les bureaux d'une école primaire depuis six ans, ce qui me plaît beaucoup. Je dois pourtant chercher un nouvel emploi parce que ça fait un peu moins de six mois que j'ai déménagé. Tous les matins, mon trajet prend plus de cinquante minutes et c'est trop long.

Je serais très motivée par le poste que vous proposez. Cela me donnerait la possibilité d'apprendre beaucoup de choses sur la routine journalière dans une maternelle. Mon fils va bientôt avoir l'âge d'entrer à la maternelle. Alors, je pourrais être assez flexible pour mes heures de travail et je serais prête à faire des heures pendant le weekend une fois de temps en temps si vous en aviez besoin.

Read these statements. Write **T** (true), **F** (false) or **?** (not mentioned in the text) in each box.

Example: Sophie read about the job on the internet.   ☐ T

(a) Sophie is applying for a job in a primary school.   ☐   *(1 mark)*

(b) She has worked in an office.   ☐   *(1 mark)*

(c) She likes her current job.   ☐   *(1 mark)*

(d) She currently walks to work.   ☐   *(1 mark)*

(e) Her journey to work takes less than 50 minutes.   ☐   *(1 mark)*

(f) Sophie has a young son.   ☐   *(1 mark)*

(g) She currently works weekends.   ☐   *(1 mark)*

(h) She would be prepared to work flexible hours.   ☐   *(1 mark)*

26 A job interview

Listen to Jacob being interviewed for a new job. Answer the questions **in English**.

Part 1

1 Where does Jacob want to work? ....   *(1 mark)*

2 What experience has he had?

....   *(1 mark)*

3 Where did he see the job advertised? ....   *(1 mark)*

Part 2

4 What does he say are his good qualities? Give **two** details.

   (a) ....   **(b)** ....   *(2 marks)*

5 When could he start the job? ....   *(1 mark)*

6 When will he be told of the decision? ....   *(1 mark)*

Job interview

27 Catherine's job interview

Read this email from Catherine about a job interview.

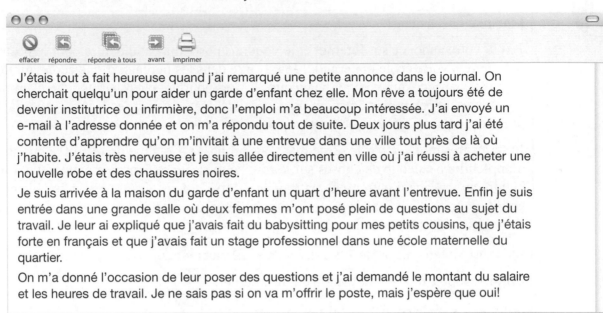

○○○

effacer répondre répondre à tous avant imprimer

J'étais tout à fait heureuse quand j'ai remarqué une petite annonce dans le journal. On cherchait quelqu'un pour aider un garde d'enfant chez elle. Mon rêve a toujours été de devenir institutrice ou infirmière, donc l'emploi m'a beaucoup intéressée. J'ai envoyé un e-mail à l'adresse donnée et on m'a répondu tout de suite. Deux jours plus tard j'ai été contente d'apprendre qu'on m'invitait à une entrevue dans une ville tout près de là où j'habite. J'étais très nerveuse et je suis allée directement en ville où j'ai réussi à acheter une nouvelle robe et des chaussures noires.

Je suis arrivée à la maison du garde d'enfant un quart d'heure avant l'entrevue. Enfin je suis entrée dans une grande salle où deux femmes m'ont posé plein de questions au sujet du travail. Je leur ai expliqué que j'avais fait du babysitting pour mes petits cousins, que j'étais forte en français et que j'avais fait un stage professionnel dans une école maternelle du quartier.

On m'a donné l'occasion de leur poser des questions et j'ai demandé le montant du salaire et les heures de travail. Je ne sais pas si on va m'offrir le poste, mais j'espère que oui!

Answer these questions **in English**.

Example:

Where did Catherine see the advert? .... *in the newspaper* ....

1 What job was advertised? .... *(1 mark)*

2 Name one of Catherine's ideal jobs. .... *(1 mark)*

3 What did Catherine do before the interview? .... *(1 mark)*

4 How early was she for the interview? .... *(1 mark)*

5 State **two** things Catherine mentioned in her interview.

  (i) ....

  (ii) .... *(2 marks)*

6 What **two** things did Catherine ask about?

  (i) ....

  (ii) .... *(2 marks)*

28 Christine's interview

Listen to Christine practising for a job interview. Answer the questions **in English**.

Example: How old is she? .... *!7* ....

1 What is her best quality? .... *(1 mark)*

2 What is her best subject at school? .... *(1 mark)*

3 Where has she already worked? .... *(1 mark)*

4 What did her employer say about her? .... *(1 mark)*

Opinions about jobs

29 Pros and cons of jobs

Read the views of jobs given here. Give an advantage and a disadvantage of each job **in English**.

Example: Être professeur est difficile car les élèves sont trop bruyants, mais c'est bien payé.

Job	Advantage	Disadvantage
Teacher	well paid	pupils too noisy

(a) Travailler comme médecin est un emploi responsable, mais les heures sont trop longues.

Job	Advantage	Disadvantage
Doctor		

(2 marks)

(b) Le travail d'hôtesse de l'air est bon car on voyage beaucoup, mais on est toujours debout.

Job	Advantage	Disadvantage
Flight attendant		

(2 marks)

(c) Travailler dans une banque est très facile mais à mon avis c'est ennuyeux.

Job	Advantage	Disadvantage
Bank worker		

(2 marks)

30 Job choices

Listen to these young people talking about jobs. Identify **the job** that each person wants to do and **the reason** why they want to do it. Write the correct letters in the boxes.

Jobs

A	nurse
B	electrician
C	police officer
D	gardener
E	baker
F	writer
G	waiter
H	engineer

Reasons

I	well paid
J	interesting
K	flexible working hours
L	varied
M	easy
N	stimulating
O	in the open air
P	help others

	Job	Reason
Example:	C	I
1		
2		
3		

(2 marks)
(2 marks)
(2 marks)

Part-time work

31 A holiday job

Read Freya's account of a holiday job.

> J'habite à la Baule qui se trouve au bord de la mer. Je n'aurais jamais pensé que mon travail d'été allait être si agréable! J'étais de bonne humeur tous les matins, avant d'aller au boulot. Comme travail, je devais m'occuper des vélos de location. Il n'y avait que moi au bureau de location. Quelle chance!
>
> Les vacanciers avaient l'habitude de louer des vélos assez tôt le matin et ils ne revenaient que vers six heures du soir, sachant que le bureau était sur le point de fermer. Pendant la journée, j'avais peu de travail, sauf aux moments rares où il y avait des choses à réparer. Alors, pour passer le temps, je me bronzais un peu sur la plage qui était à moins de vingt mètres. J'étais très contente de bavarder avec les visiteurs qui passaient et de les conseiller sur les endroits intéressants qu'ils pourraient visiter.
>
> En fin de journée, une chose qui était embêtante pour moi, c'était de laver tous les vélos avant de fermer le bureau de location.

Which of these statements are true? Write the correct **five** letters in the boxes.

A	La Baule is on the coast.
B	Freya always thought that her holiday job was going to be great fun.
C	She sold bikes to tourists.
D	She worked on her own.
E	The tourists always came back early.
F	Freya was not very busy during the day.
G	She spent lots of time repairing bikes.
H	She told the visitors good places to see on holiday.
I	She had no time for sunbathing.
J	She had to clean the bikes at the end of the day.

☐ *(1 mark)*   ☐ *(1 mark)*   ☐ *(1 mark)*   ☐ *(1 mark)*   ☐ *(1 mark)*

32 What jobs do they do?

Listen to these young people talking about part-time jobs. What does each person do? Write the correct letter in each box.

A	Stacking shelves		E	Delivering newspapers
B	Working in a restaurant		F	Working in a sports centre
C	Washing cars		G	Working on a farm
D	Doing housework		H	Babysitting

Example: H

1 ☐ *(1 mark)*   **2** ☐ *(1 mark)*   **3** ☐ *(1 mark)*   **4** ☐ *(1 mark)*

Work experience

B READING

33 Thierry's work experience

Read Thierry's email about work experience.

⊘ effacer   ↩ répondre   ↩ répondre à tous   ➔ avant   🖨 imprimer

J'ai fait mon stage dans un bureau au centre-ville. Chaque jour, j'y allais en bus parce que j'habite assez loin du centre. Le stage n'a duré qu'une semaine et j'étais un peu nerveux avant de commencer, mais le patron était sympa et mes collègues étaient vraiment gentils aussi, alors tout s'est très bien passé.

Je faisais des photocopies, je préparais le café et je mettais des données dans l'ordinateur. Un jour, je suis allé dans une entreprise de la ville voisine avec mon patron qui a réussi à vendre des articles au patron de cette entreprise.

Le dernier jour, on m'a donné un stylo comme souvenir de mon stage. Le stage était agréable mais je sais que je n'aimerais pas travailler dans un bureau à l'avenir.

Read these statements. Write **T** (true), **F** (false) or **?** (not mentioned in the text) in each box.

Example: Thierry did his work experience in an office.   [T]

(a) He lives close to the office.   ☐   *(1 mark)*

(b) The work experience lasted a week.   ☐   *(1 mark)*

(c) He already knew the boss.   ☐   *(1 mark)*

(d) He enjoyed the work experience.   ☐   *(1 mark)*

(e) He never left the office during the work experience.   ☐   *(1 mark)*

(f) He would like to work in an office in the future.   ☐   *(1 mark)*

F LISTENING 83

34 Where did they work?

Listen to these young people talking about work experience. Where did each person work? Write the correct letter in each box.

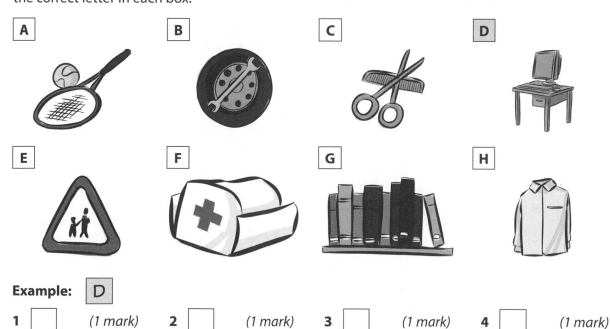

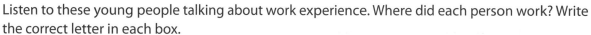

Example: [D]

1 ☐   *(1 mark)*   **2** ☐   *(1 mark)*   **3** ☐   *(1 mark)*   **4** ☐   *(1 mark)*

My work experience

35 My work experience

Match the sentence halves so that each complete sentence makes sense in French. Write the correct letter in each box.

- In tasks like this, make sure the two halves of the sentence work together and make sense.

- Take care with negatives. If the first half of the sentence ends with *ne* or *n'*, the other part of the negative (often *pas*) must be present in the second half.

- Try translating each complete sentence into English to check that it does make sense.

a	Le travail était …
b	Je m'entendais bien …
c	Ce n'était …
d	Il y avait beaucoup …
e	Mon stage a duré …
f	Mes collègues étaient …
g	Mon patron m'a montré …

A	à faire.
B	quinze jours.
C	très gentils.
D	trop de travail.
E	avec mes collègues.
F	bien organisé.
G	des problèmes.
H	pas du tout difficile.
I	comment entrer des données dans la base des données.

(a) ☐ *(1 mark)*   **(e)** ☐ *(1 mark)*

(b) ☐ *(1 mark)*   **(f)** ☐ *(1 mark)*

(c) ☐ *(1 mark)*   **(g)** ☐ *(1 mark)*

(d) ☐ *(1 mark)*

36 How was their work experience?

Listen to these people talking about work experience. What are their opinions? Write **P** (positive), **N** (negative) or **P/N** (both positive and negative) in each box.

Example: | P |

1	☐	*(1 mark)*
2	☐	*(1 mark)*
3	☐	*(1 mark)*
4	☐	*(1 mark)*
5	☐	*(1 mark)*
6	☐	*(1 mark)*
7	☐	*(1 mark)*

If you find it difficult to identify positive and negative opinions, listen out for linking words such as *cependant* and *pourtant* (both of which mean 'however'). Words like this suggest that there are two parts to the answer, one positive and one negative.

Articles 1

To say 'the' in French you use *le, la, l'* or *les* In front of the noun. Remember that in French every noun has a gender. Objects are either masculine (m) or feminine (f) and are singular or plural.

A Put in the correct word for 'the' (*le, la, l', les*) in front of these nouns. They are all places around a town.

Example: banque (f) *La banque*

1 .... commerces (pl)	**5** .... cinémas (pl)	**9** .... rues (pl)
2 .... pharmacie (f)	**6** .... bowling (m)	**10** .... appartement (m)
3 .... toilettes (pl)	**7** .... gare (f)	
4 .... hôtel (m)	**8** .... parking (m)	

B Here is a list of animals. Put the correct word for 'the' in front of the noun.

1 .... chienne (f)	**5** .... tortue (f)	**9** .... mouche (f)
2 .... serpents (pl)	**6** .... éléphant (m)	**10** .... cochons d'Inde (pl)
3 .... araignée (f)	**7** .... poissons (pl)	**11** .... grenouille (f)
4 .... chat (m)	**8** .... canard (m)	**12** .... singe (m)

To say 'a' or 'an' in French, you use *un* or *une* depending on whether the noun is masculine or feminine.

C Show that you understand when to put in *un* or *une* in front of these parts of a house.

1 .... salon	**4** .... chambre	**7** .... salle à manger
2 .... salle de bains	**5** .... sous-sol	
3 .... jardin	**6** .... cuisine	

D Fill in the gaps in this table, paying attention to the articles: *un, une, des, le, la, l', les*.

Singular	Plural
	les chiens
un château	
l'animal	
	des voitures
le nez	
le bateau	
un hôtel	
l'arbre	les arbres
	des pages
	les eaux
une araignée	
	les destinations

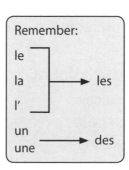

Remember:

le
la   → les
l'

un
une   → des

Articles 2

> If you want to say 'some' or 'any' in French, you use the partitive article *du, de la, des* or *de l'*, depending on the gender of the noun you are talking about.

A Put the correct word for 'some' in front of these nouns. Pay attention to the gender given in brackets.

Example: farine (f)   de la farine (some flour)

1 .... œufs (pl)   **5** .... eau minérale (f)   **9** .... huile (f)

2 .... confiture (f)   **6** .... jambon (m)   **10** .... riz (m)

3 .... pain (m)   **7** .... frites (pl)

4 .... haricots verts (pl)   **8** .... crème (f)

B Fill in the gaps below, using *du / de la / des / de l'* in order to ask your friend if they want any of the items:

Tu veux ..*des*.. pâtes, ... abricots, ... fromage, ... chocolat, ... olives, ... porc, ... pommes de terre, ... ketchup, ... ananas, ... potage, ... œufs, ... sel et .... poivre?

C Unfortunately, you have nothing left to eat in the house. Using the example below, answer the following questions, then translate into English.

> Always use *de* after a negative in French to say 'some' or 'any'.

Example: Tu as des pommes? ..... *Je n'ai pas de pommes.   I don't have any apples.* ....

1 Tu as de l'argent? ....

2 Tu as du pain? ....

3 Tu as des céréales? ....

4 Tu as de la pizza? ....

D Re-read all the rules and fill in the gaps with *du, de la, de l', des* or *de*.

Tu as .... fruits et .... légumes? Oui, j'ai .... fruits mais je n'ai pas .... légumes. Par exemple, j'ai .... pêches et .... cerises mais je n'ai pas .... carottes ni .... pommes de terre. Cependant, j'ai .... pain et .... nutella, donc on peut manger .... sandwichs.

> You use *au, à la, à l'* or *aux* to translate 'to the'.

E Using *au, à la, à l'* or *aux*, fill in the gaps to tell your friend where you are going in town this afternoon.

Example: Je vais ...*au*... cinéma,

1 Je vais .... patinoire.   **4** Je vais .... hôtel de ville.

2 Je vais .... crêperie.   **5** Je vais .... magasins.

3 Je vais .... théâtre.   **6** Je vais .... café-tabac.

F Say what part of the house you are going to, using *Je vais au / à la / à l' / aux* ...

1 .... salon   **7** .... atelier

2 .... cuisine   **8** .... grenier

3 .... salle de bains   **9** .... cave

4 .... chambres   **10** .... entrée

5 .... salle de jeux   **11** .... garage

6 .... jardin   **12** .... salle à manger

Adjectives

Adjectives are used to describe nouns. Remember that in French you need to ensure they have the correct endings depending on whether the noun is masculine, feminine, singular or plural.

A Circle the correct form of the adjectives.

1 Ma mère est petit / petite.

2 Mon père est grand / grande.

3 Ma maison est beau / belle.

4 Mon chat est noir / noire.

5 Elle est heureux / heureuse.

6 Les fenêtres sont chère /chères.

B Using the adjectives in the box, complete the sentences below. Don't forget to change them to the feminine or plural form where necessary.

1 Mon chien est .... (sad)

2 Mes crayons sont .... (white)

3 Ma mère est .... (intelligent)

4 Mes frères sont .... (shy)

5 Mes sœurs sont .... (fat)

6 Ma chatte est très .... (cute)

gros
blanc
timide
mignon
triste
intelligent

C Complete this table with all the different forms of the adjectives.

masc sing.	fem. sing.	masc. plural	fem. plural	English
grand	grande		grandes	big/tall
	petite			
noir		noirs		
	neuve		neuves	
		derniers		last
marron		marron		
triste		tristes		sad
sérieux		sérieux		
	gentille		gentilles	kind
	sèche	secs		
drôle		drôles		funny
	vieille		vieilles	old
	belle	beaux		
ancien		anciens		ancient
blanc		blancs		white
	sportive		sportives	

D Make sentences that use the adjectives in **C** above. Make sure they have the correct form and are in the correct position.

Example: J'ai deux chattes (grand, noir) *J'ai deux grandes chattes noires.*

1 Elle a de yeux (beau, bleu). ....

2 Les fleurs (meilleur, jaune). ....

3 Mes baskets (vieux, blanc). ....

4 Mes parents (pauvre, malade). ....

Most adjectives come **after** the noun but some come **before**, e.g. grand

Possessives

To say something is 'my', 'your', 'his', etc, you use a possessive adjective e.g. *mon. ma, mes.*

A 1 Choose *mon, ma* or *mes* to fill in the gaps.

Dans ...ma... famille, il y a .... père, ... mère, ... sœur et .... deux frères. .... grand-mère vient souvent nous rendre visite avec .... grand-père. .... amie adore .... grands-parents et elle vient jouer avec toutes .... affaires quand ils sont là.

2 Use *son / sa / ses* to fill in the gaps.

Dans ...sa... chambre, elle a .... lit, ... livres, ... bureau, ... télévision, ... bijoux, ... téléphone et .... nounours.

3 Use *notre / notre / nos* to translate 'our' or *votre / votre / vos* to translate 'your'.

Dans .....notre...... collège, nous avons .... professeurs, ... bibliothèque, ... cantine, et .... terrain de sport. Et vous, qu'est-ce que vous avez dans .... collège et dans .... salles de classe? Vous avez .... tableaux blancs interactifs et .... gymnase?

4 Your teacher asks you questions about yourself. Insert the correct word for 'your'.

(a) Comment s'appellent .... père et .... mère?

(b) Qu'est-ce que tu achètes avec .... argent?

(c) C'est quand .... anniversaire?

(d) Qu'est-ce qu'il y a dans .... ville ou .... village?

5 How would you talk about what they have in **their** village?

Dans .....leur..... village, ils ont .... mairie, ... cinémas, ... pharmacie, ... boulangerie, ... cafés, ... parcs, ... hôpital, ... école et tous .... petits commerces.

B How many grammatically correct but silly sentences can you make from this table?

mon / ma / mes	fromage			jaune(s)
ton / ta / tes	copines	est		honnête(s)
son / sa / ses	vélo	n'est pas	très	moderne(s)
notre / nos	gâteaux	sont	assez	grand(e)(s)
votre / vos	football	ne sont pas		timide(s)
leur / leurs	photos			romantique(s)

....

....

....

....

....

C These clothes all belong to you. Say so!

1 La chemise? .....C'est la mienne!...

2 Les pulls? Ce sont ....

3 Les jupes? Ce sont ....

4 Le jogging? C'est ....

To say something is 'mine', use *le / la* or *les + mien(ne)(s)*. For example: *La chemise, c'est la mienne.*

Comparisons

> Use the comparative form of the adjective to say 'more than' or 'less than':
> *plus* + adjective + *que* or *moins* + adjective + *que*
> Use the superlative form of the adjective to say 'the most' or 'the least':
> *le / la / les* + *plus / moins* + adjective
> The adjective ending must agree with the noun it refers to.

A Work out who is the most and the least intelligent, Marie, Lydie or Paul.

Marie est intelligente.

Marie est plus intelligente que Paul.

Paul est moins intelligent que Lydie.

Lydie est plus intelligente que Marie.

Paul n'est pas aussi intelligent que Marie.

> Some comparatives and superlatives are irregular:
> *pire* = worse (*le / la pire* = the worst)
> *meilleur* = better (*le / la meilleur* = the best)

Qui est le / la plus intelligent(e)? ....

Qui est le / la moins intelligent(e)? ....

B Using the grades below, make up four sentences about who is the better student in each subject.

Example: .....Antoine est meilleur en anglais qu'Anna. ....

	Antoine	Anna	
Anglais	D	B	....
Français	A	C	....
Géo	C	E	....
Dessin	B	A*	....

C Put each of these sentences in the correct order, then translate them.

Example: est que courte plus jupe Ma jupe ta   .....Ma jupe est plus courte que ta jupe. ....

.....My skirt is shorter than your skirt. ....

1 aussi est Sara grand Philippe que ....

2 maths que plus musique Les difficiles sont la ....

3 Les moins sont les sains fruits bonbons que ....

4 Une est moins un confortable cravate qu' jogging ....

5 l' chimie que est intéressante aussi anglais La ....

D Use the adjective given, with *le / la / les plus* to make a superlative sentence. Make sure the adjective matches the noun.

Example: Le TGV est le train … (rapide) ....Le TGV est le train le plus rapide. ....

1 Les kiwis sont les fruits … (sain) ....

2 L'hiver est la saison … (froid) ....

3 Londres est … (grand) ville d'Angleterre. ....

Now use the adjective given, with *le / la / les moins* to say 'the least'.

Example: Voilà la cathédrale … (traditionnel) ....Voilà la cathédrale la moins traditionnelle. ...

4 Où sont les garçons … (actif)? ....

5 Je prends les vêtements … (long) ....

6 J'habite dans la région … (industriel) ....

Other adjectives

A Say which clothes you are going to wear on holiday, using *ce, cet, cette* or *ces*.

Je vais porter …

Example: pull ......*ce pull*............................

1 pantalon	**5** anorak....................................
2 imperméable	**6** sandales ....
3 robe	**7** chaussettes............................
4 baskets	**8** jupe.......................................

> *ce* = this (m)
> *cet* = this in front of a masculine noun beginning with a vowel)
> *cette* = this (f)
> *ces* = these (plu)

B Say you always prefer the one(s) on the left, using *celui, celle, ceux* or *celles*.
(You get a clue to the gender by looking at the spelling of 'which' at the beginning.)

Example: Quelle jupe préfères-tu?   Je préfère .....*celle*.......... à gauche.

1 Quel livre préfères-tu?   Je préfère .... à gauche.

2 Quels garçons préfères-tu?   Je préfère .... à gauche.

3 Quelle salle préfères-tu?   Je préfère .... à gauche.

4 Quelles cartes postales préfères-tu?   Je préfère .... à gauche.

> *celui* (m) / *celle* (f) = the one
> *ceux* (m)/*celles* (f) = those

C Complete the question by asking your friend if they prefer this one here, that one there, these or those.

Example: Quels bateaux préfères-tu? .....*Ceux-ci ou ceux-là?*.........................

1 Quel stylo préfères-tu? ....

2 Quelle station balnéaire préfères-tu? ....

3 Quelles ceintures préfères-tu? ....

4 Quels hôtels préfères-tu? ....

> You add on -*ci* when you want to say' here'.
> You add -*là* when you want to say 'there'.

D You don't hear what they say, so you have to ask your friend which one(s) they prefer yet again.

Use *lequel, laquelle, lesquels* or *lesquelles* to repeat each question in exercise C.

Example: Quels bateaux préfères-tu? .....*Lesquels?*...............................

1 Quel stylo préfères-tu?..

2 Quelle station balnéaire préfères-tu? ....

3 Quelles ceintures préfères-tu? ....

4 Quels hôtels préfères-tu? ....

> *lequel* (m) / *laquelle* (f) = which one?

E Fill in the missing words as shown in the example.

Example: Quel appartement préfères-tu? Celui-ci ou celui-là? Lequel?

1 .... cuisine préfères-tu? Celle-ci ou .... Laquelle?

2 Quelles cravates préfères-tu? .... ou celles-là? ....?

3 .... jardin préfères-tu? .... ou ....?
Lequel?

4 .... gants préfères-tu? .... ou ....?
.................................?

Adverbs

Adverbs are used to describe the verb. In French a lot of adverbs end in **-ment**.

A Form adverbs from these adjectives.

Example: heureux ......heureusement..........

1 doux ....

2 naturel ....

3 absolu ....

4 général ....

5 attentif ....

6 vrai ....

7 lent ....

8 gentil ....

B Underline all the adverbs in this paragraph, then translate it. Use the English translations in the box if you are stuck.

> first
> often
> then
> finally
> in the future

Le matin, <u>d'abord</u>, je me lève à sept heures, puis d'habitude je prends mon petit déjeuner. Ensuite, je quitte la maison et finalement j'arrive au collège à huit heures et demie. Mais c'est souvent trop tôt. Alors à l'avenir je vais rester au lit plus longtemps.

.....In the morning...

....

....

....

C Fill in the gaps from this passage with the best adverb from the box. There may be more than one answer. The first letter of the adverb has been given for you.

absolument, d'abord, de temps en temps, ~~généralement,~~ par conséquent, régulièrement, sans doute, seulement, souvent, toujours, vraiment

...Généralement... je vais en France avec mes parents et mon petit frère pour les grandes vacances. S........................... mes grands-parents viennent avec nous, et d'........................... c'est v........................... pratique car ils font r........................... du baby-sitting. Cependant, de ...., ils se sentent v........................... fatigués et ils ne sont pas t........................... confortables. P........................... ils ne viendront pas l'année prochaine. À l'avenir, ils viendront s........................... s'ils sont a........................... en bonne forme!

D Complete these sentences using adverbs from the box.

1 Je conduis (always) très (carefully).

   .....Je conduis toujours très attentivement.....................

2 (Usually) il fait la vaisselle (straight away).

   ....

3 (From time to time) elle écoute de la musique (quietly).

   ....

4 Ma valise? (Naturally) j'avais laissé mes vêtements (inside).

   ....

> ~~attentivement~~
> d'habitude
> ~~toujours~~
> doucement
> dedans
> tout de suite
> naturellement
> de temps en temps

E Write four sentences of your own with at least one adverb in each.

....

....

....

....

Object pronouns

Direct object pronouns are words like 'it', 'me', 'him', 'us', etc. You use them when you don't want to keep repeating a noun or a name.

A Translate these sentences.

Example: Il me regarde. ..He watches me......

1 Nous te voyons. ....
2 Tu le connais? ....
3 Je veux la voir. ....

4 Vous nous rencontrez. ....
5 Elle vous oubliera. ....
6 Je les perdrai. ....

You use **indirect** object pronouns to replace a noun which has *à* (*au*, *aux*, etc.) in front of it.

B Translate the following sentences. Notice that in English we sometimes omit the 'to'

Example: Il me donne un billet. ....He gives me a ticket. / He gives a ticket to me................

1 Je te passe mes bonbons. ....
2 Ne lui dis pas la vérité. ....
3 Nous lui offrirons un bateau. ....
4 Il va nous envoyer un cadeau. ....
5 Tu leur raconteras l'histoire. ....

> 'Him', 'her' and 'them' are translated as *lui* or *leur*.

C Put the words in the correct order to answer the question.

Example: Tu aimes les pommes? je beaucoup aime les Oui .....Oui, je les aime beaucoup..........

1 Vous comprenez le professeur?   le souvent comprenons Nous

....

2 Elle aime les sports nautiques?   pas aime Elle ne du tout les

....

3 Tu vas vendre ton vélo?   vendre vais le Oui je demain

....

4 Il veut acheter la maison?   veut pas il acheter ne Non l'

....

D Replace the noun with a pronoun and move it to the correct position in the sentence.

Example: J'ai mangé le gâteau. .....Je l'ai mangé..

1 Il cherche les clefs. ....
2 Nous envoyons un cadeau à Jeanne. ....
3 Il a donné des bonbons aux enfants. ....
4 Tu as téléphoné à tes amis? ....
5 Elle dit toujours la vérité à papa. ....

E Complete the following sentences.

Example: I'm sending it to you. Je .....vous l'..... envoie.

1 She offered them to us. Elle .... a offerts.
2 Don't sell them to him/her! Ne .... vends pas!
3 I am going to pass it(m) to you. Je vais .... passer.
4 He gave them to you on Saturday. Il .... a donnés samedi.

Other pronouns: *y* and *en*

> You use *y* to refer to a place which has already been mentioned. It often means 'there': *Il adore* **Paris**. *Il* **y** *est allé hier.* You also use it with verbs that take *à*.

A Replace the nouns with the pronoun *y.*

Example: Tu vas au cinéma ce soir? ..... *Tu y vas ce soir?* .....

1 Il va habiter **au Canada**. ....

2 Elle a vu ses amis **en France**. ....

3 Vous jouez **au tennis**? ....

4 J'ai réussi **mon examen**. ....

5 Tu es allée **au travail** ce matin? ....

> You use *en* to replace a noun. It often means 'of it', 'of them' or 'some':
> *J'aime* **le chocolat**. *J'en mange beaucoup.*

B Unjumble these sentences with *en* in order to answer the questions.

Example: Tu as de l'argent?   ai j' Oui en ..... *Oui j'en ai* .....

1 Tu fais beaucoup de sport?   en beaucoup J' fais ....

2 Elle fait du ski?   pas en fait n'Elle ....

3 Vous avez deux frères?   trois ai Non en j' ....

4 Ils mangent de la pizza tous les jours?   les en samedis Ils tous mangent ....

5 Il y a des bouteilles dans la cave?   y en Il a plusieurs ....

C Replace the nouns in brackets with either *y* or *en*.

1 Je vais [au restaurant] de temps en temps.

....

2 J'adore les fruits et je mange beaucoup [de fruits].

....
....

3 Ma faiblesse, c'est le chocolat, mais je ne mange jamais [de chocolat], parce que je ne veux pas grossir.

....
....

4 Je suis allé [au théâtre] la semaine dernière, avec mon frère.

....
....

5 On va au concert ce soir. Tu veux aller [au concert] avec nous?

....
....

6 Moi, j'adore le poulet, mais mon frère ne mange pas [le poulet], parce qu'il est végétarien.

....
....

> Using pronouns makes your work more interesting and for your GCSE, if you are aiming for higher grades, you should try and use them.

Other pronouns

> Relative pronouns are used when you want to link statements together to avoid repetition and to make your French more fluent.

A Fill in the gaps with *qui* (followed by a verb), or *que / qu'* (followed by a subject / person).

> *Qui* means 'which', 'who' or 'that' and replaces the subject in the clause it introduces.
> *Que* means 'whom', 'which' or 'that' and replaces the object in the clause.

Example: C'est le bruit ......*que*...... je n'aime pas.

1 Le repas .... j'ai pris, était excellent.
2 C'est Claude .... est le plus beau.
3 Ce sont mes parents .... adorent la viande.
4 Voilà le chapeau .... il a perdu.
5 Où sont les robes .... sont déchirées?
6 L'église .... j'ai visitée était vieille / ancienne.
7 L'homme .... monte dans le train est gros.
8 Ma copine .... s'appelle Mathilde a seize ans.
9 Quel est le film .... tu veux voir?

B Translate the following sentences carefully once you have inserted *dont*.

> *Dont* replaces 'whose' or 'of whom / which' for example:
> *Je veux voir le film **dont** j'ai vu la bande-annonce.*
> I want to see the film of which I saw the trailer.

Example: La personne ......*dont*...... je parlais n'est plus là.

.....The person I was talking about is no longer there.....

1 La vie .... vous rêvez n'existe pas.

....

2 Les papiers .... j'ai besoin sont dans le tiroir.

....

3 Je ne connais pas la maladie .... tu souffres.

....

4 Ce garçon .... je te parlais a quitté le collège.

....

C Which would you use: *y, en, où, qui, que* or *dont*? Insert the correct pronoun and translate into English.

1 Le repas .... nous avons mangé était excellent.

....

2 Le stylo .... vous avez besoin, est cassé.

....

3 Des bonbons? J'........................... ai mangé beaucoup.

....

4 Le café .... je vais le samedi est fermé.

....

5 Le cinéma Gaumont? J'........................... suis allée pour voir 'Amélie'.

....

Present tense: -ER verbs

A Give the *je, nous* and *ils* forms of each of these verbs.

Verb	je (j')	nous	ils
aimer	j'aime	nous aimons	ils aiment
jouer			
habiter			
regarder			
donner			
inviter			
marcher			
trouver			
voler			
garder			

B Use the verbs above to write how you would say:

Example: he likes   il aime

1 you (pl) keep ....
2 she invites ....
3 you (s) live ....
4 we find ....

5 he looks at ....
6 you (pl) walk ....
7 you (s) give ....
8 she steals ....

9 he plays ....
10 they look at ....

> Although the verbs below are -er verbs, they are slightly irregular in that the spelling often changes, for example *manger* becomes *mangeons* in the *nous* form.

C Put the verbs in brackets in the correct form and watch out for the spelling.

-ger verbs

1 ils (ranger) ....
2 nous (plonger) ....
3 nous (nager) ....
4 je (manger) ....

-ler / -ter verbs

1 je (s'appeler) ....
2 ils (jeter) ....
3 nous (se rappeler) ....
4 elle (projeter) ....

-yer verbs

5 tu (envoyer) ....
6 vous (payer) ....
7 j'(essayer) ....
8 nous (nettoyer) ....

acheter type verbs

5 tu (acheter) ....
6 elles (préférer) ....
7 vous (se lever) ....
8 il (geler) ....

D Fill in the correct part of the verb in these questions and translate them.

Example: Tu (parler) français?   Tu parles français? Do you speak French?

2 Ils (habiter) en France? ....
3 Marie (ranger) sa chambre? ....
4 Vous (préférer) les sciences? ....
5 Les sœurs (jeter) les fruits? ....
6 Mon copain et moi (acheter) des frites? ....

95

-IR and -RE verbs

-ir and *-re* verbs are another set of verbs which follow a regular pattern. It is important to learn the most common verbs.

A What do these *-ir* verbs mean? Match the English to the French.

choisir	to warn
réfléchir	to slow down
ralentir	to punish
rougir	to finish
finir	to blush
punir	to think about
atterrir	to land
avertir	to choose

B Fill in the gaps in this table. (The verbs are irregular.)

	dormir	sortir
je		sors
tu	dors	
il/elle		sort
nous		
vous		sortez
ils	dorment	

> Be careful, many of the *-ir* verbs like *choisir* and *finir* add *-is, -is, -it, -issons, -issez, -issent*.

C Put the correct ending on these *-ir* verbs to make them match their subjects.

Example: Ils (avertir) les garçons. .....Ils avertissent les garçons...

1 L'ami (choisir) un cadeau. ....

2 Vous (courir) aux magasins. ....

3 Nous (finir) nos devoirs. ....

4 Je (remplir) le verre de vin. ....

D Complete the table below.

	vendre	prendre	dire
je			
tu	vends		
il/elle			
nous		prenons	disons
vous		prenez	
ils/elles	vendent		

E Give the correct present tense of the verb in brackets.

1 nous (vendre) ....

2 ils (répondre) ....

3 je (descendre) ....

4 tu (prendre) ....

5 vous (boire) ....

6 elle (lire) ....

7 j' (écrire) ....

8 il (comprendre) ....

avoir and *être*

A Give the correct part of *avoir* in these sentences.

Example: Tu ....*as*........ un frère?

1 Elle .... un hamster.

2 J'.................... les cheveux blonds.

3 Ils .... une grande maison.

4 Il .... onze ans.

5 Nous .... un petit gymnase.

6 Vous .... un beau chien.

7 Ma sœur .... une jupe rouge.

8 Les filles .... un piercing.

9 Tu .... deux guitares.

10 Vous .... une nouvelle maison.

B Translate the following sentences into French.

Example: We have a house in Angers.   .....*Nous avons une maison à Angers*...........................

1 They have a dog and three hamsters.   ....

2 Do you have a sister?   ....

3 She has black hair.   ....

4 We have a big kitchen.   ....

5 I have three children.   ....

6 I am sixteen years old.   ....

7 He has a car.   ....

C Fill in the gaps with the correct part of *être*.

Example: Il est très amusant.

1 Je .... français.

2 Nous .... paresseux.

3 Ma tante .... assez petite.

4 Vous .... sportif mais timide.

5 Mes yeux .... bleus.

6 Tu .... célibataire?

7 Les chiens .... mignons.

8 Je .... au chômage.

9 Nous .... mariés.

10 Il .... paresseux.

D Write six sentences using *être* or *avoir* and words from the grid below.

Je	maison	bouclés	petit
Tu	yeux	bleu	professeur
L'homme	grand	amusant	court
Nos chiens	mariés	cheveux	piercing
Vos parents	rouge	voiture	marron
Les filles	triste	long	gros

....

....

....

....

....

....

> Remember, when you are using the verb *être* you need to make sure the adjective agrees with the noun!

97

aller and *faire*

> *Faire* and *aller* are two other important irregular verbs. They mean 'to do' and 'to go'.

A Give the right form of the verb *aller* to complete each sentence.

Example: Il ___va___ à la bibliothèque.

1 Les jeunes _____ au centre commercial.
2 Je _____ au marché samedi.
3 Vous _____ sortir ce soir?
4 Maman _____ à l'église.
5 Où _____-tu vendredi soir?

6 Les chiens _____ dans le garage.
7 Les parents _____ au restaurant.
8 Marc _____ au centre sportif.
9 Nous _____ en France pour nos vacances.
10 Je _____ au collège.

B What jobs are they doing? Fill in the gaps with the right part of *faire* and say what each one means in English.

Example: Mon père ___fait___ les lits.   ___My dad makes the beds.___

1 Mon frère _____ la vaisselle.   _____
2 Mes sœurs _____ tout le ménage.   _____
3 Vous _____ le repassage.   _____
4 Nous _____ la cuisine.   _____
5 Ils _____ le jardinage.   _____
6 Je _____ la lessive.   _____
7 Maman _____ les courses.   _____
8 Tu _____ du shopping.   _____

C Which sports are they all doing? Put in the correct part of *faire*.

Example: Je ___fais___ du cyclisme.

1 Ma sœur _____ de la danse.
2 Nous _____ des randonnées.
3 Ils _____ du ski nautique.
4 Tu _____ de la gymnastique.

5 Vous _____ de la danse?
6 Elles _____ de l'équitation.
7 Nous _____ de la planche à voile.
8 Il _____ de l'escalade.

D Now choose whether you need a part of *aller* or *faire* to complete each sentence.

1 Jean _____ à la pêche.
2 Nous _____ de la voile tous les samedis.
3 Vous _____ du basket.
4 Ils _____ à la montagne pour faire du ski.
5 Tu _____ au concert samedi soir?
6 Ils _____ de l'athlétisme.
7 Elle _____ souvent au cinéma.
8 Je _____ faire des promenades.
9 Tu _____ du skate?
10 Mes camarades _____ du vélo.

Modal verbs

The verbs *devoir* (to have to / must), *pouvoir* (to be able to / can), *vouloir* (to want to) and *savoir* (to know) are known as **modal verbs**.

A Complete this table with the correct part of the modal verb.

	devoir	**pouvoir**	**vouloir**	**savoir**
je	dois			sais
tu		peux		
il/elle/on			veut	
nous	devons			savons
vous			voulez	
ils/elles		peuvent		

B Rearrange the words to make correct sentences.

Example: la dois prendre Je première rue ...... *Je dois prendre la première rue.* ....

1 mon -vous Pouvez père aider? ....

2 nager -tu Sais? ....

3 maison acheter parents une veulent Mes nouvelle ....

....

4 s'arrêter feux On toujours doit aux rouges ....

....

5 moi avec ce Voulez danser soir -vous? ....

....

6 sais allemand français Je et parler ....

C Change the verb to match the new subject given in italics.

Example: Il doit travailler dur et moi aussi, *je* ...... *dois travailler dur* ....

1 Elle veut trouver une chambre avec un balcon et nous aussi, *nous* ....

2 Les élèves peuvent louer un vélo et toi aussi, *tu* ....

3 Le pilote doit tout vérifier et vous aussi, *vous* ....

4 Elle sait faire la cuisine, et eux aussi, *ils* ....

5 Je peux faire un pique-nique et elles aussi, *elles* ....

6 Il ne peut jamais comprendre les régles et vous aussi, *vous* ....

7 Nous savons préparer le dîner et moi aussi, *je* ....

D Make up six sentences about school from this table.

	(ne) doit (pas)	manger en classe.
		porter ses propres vêtements.
	(ne) peut (pas)	courir dans les couloirs.
On		répondre aux professeurs.
	(ne) veut (pas)	dormir en classe.
		lancer les cahiers dans l'air.
	(ne) sait (pas)	faire des piercings aux autres élèves.
		envoyer des textos.

Reflexive verbs

A Add the correct reflexive pronoun to this verse, do the actions, then try and learn it.

Je .... lève

Tu .... laves

Il .... brosse les dents

Je ....'habille et après

Je prends mon petit déjeuner.

> **se laver – to wash oneself**
> je me lave
> tu te laves
> il / elle / on se lave
> nous nous lavons
> vous vous lavez
> ils / elles se lavent

B Add the correct reflexive pronoun.

Mes parents ...... se ...... réveillent tôt le matin. Je .... appelle Lydie. Le matin

je .... réveille à 7 heures et demie mais je ne .... lève pas tout de suite.

Normalement ma sœur .... lève à 8 heures. Nous .... lavons dans la salle de

bains et nous .... habillons vite. Après le petit déjeuner, nous .... dépêchons

pour prendre le bus au collège. On .... approche du collège et on est très contentes. Vous

.... amusez bien à votre collège?

C Write the numbers of these sentences in the correct order to match your morning routine.

1 Je me douche et je m'habille.

2 Je me réveille et je me lève.

3 J'arrive au collège et je m'amuse bien au collège.

4 Je me dépêche pour prendre mon petit déjeuner et quitter la maison.

....

D Complete the table with verbs in the present and perfect tense. Remember to use *être* with reflexive verbs.

Present	Perfect
1 je	je me suis reposé(e)
2 elle se douche	elle
3 nous	nous nous sommes amusé(e)s
4 elles s'étonnent	elles
5 vous	vous vous êtes dépêché(e)(s)

E Circle the correct part of the verb to complete the sentence.

1 Je me *est / suis / es* reposée à 8 heures ce matin.

2 Nous nous *êtes / sont / sommes* dépêchés pour aller au match.

3 Ma sœur ne s'est pas *douché / douchée / douchées* hier soir.

4 Mes deux frères se *ont / sont / était* bien entendus en vacances.

5 Vous vous êtes *couchée / couchés / couché* tôt samedi, mes amis?

6 Les garçons se sont *disputé / disputées / disputés*.

The perfect tense 1

> You use the perfect tense to talk about single events in the past. It is formed by using the present tense of *avoir* + past participle.

A Create your own sentences using a word or words from each column.

J'ai	fini	le gâteau
Tu as	détesté	le bateau
Il a	vendu	les devoirs
Elle a	regardé	l'argent
Nous avons	lavé	la maison
Vous avez	attendu	l'autobus
Ils ont	choisi	les chiens
Elles ont	perdu	le pain

....

....

....

....

....

....

....

....

B Add the correct part of *avoir* to complete these sentences.

Example: J'....ai........... regardé la télé samedi soir.

1 Mme Blanc .... invité sa copine au match.

2 Vous .... terminé le repas?

3 Ils .... fumé une cigarette.

4 Il .... beaucoup neigé ce matin.

5 Tu n'................... pas mangé de légumes?

6 Nous .... choisi un bon restaurant.

7 Elle n'................... pas rougi.

8 Ils .... atterri à l'aéroport d'Orly.

9 J'................... rendu visite à ma tante.

10 Nous n'................... pas entendu.

C Did you notice the position of the *ne … pas* in exercise B to say that they did **not** do something? Using the table in exercise A to help you, how would you say the following?

Example: You (s) did not sell the house. .....Tu n'as pas vendu la maison.................

1 We did not lose the money. ....

2 They did not wash the bus. ....

3 You (pl) did not wait for the dogs. ....

4 I did not finish the bread. ....

5 She did not sell the boat. ....

6 He did not hate the homework. ....

D Revise the irregular past participles, then fill in the gaps in these sentences.

Example: Il a .....vu........... la voiture. (voir)

1 J'ai .... le pique-nique par terre. ....

2 Elle a .... à son frère. (écrire)

3 Tu n'as rien .... au collège? (faire)

4 Il n'a pas .... ma lettre. (lire)

5 Nous avons .... acheter une Renault. (pouvoir)

E Complete these sentences with part of *avoir* and the past participle of the verb given.

1 J'................... la situation. (comprendre)

2 Il .... de rentrer vite. (promettre)

3 Tu .... un taxi à la gare? (prendre)

4 Qu'est-ce que tu .... (faire)

The perfect tense 2

> The perfect tense can also be formed using the verb *être* + past participle, when the verb is reflexive and with 13 verbs of movement.

A Add the correct part of the verb *être* to complete these sentences.

Example: Tu ......*es*........ né en 2000?

1 Elle .... tombée par terre.

2 Mes copains .... arrivés trop tard.

3 Les chats .... montés sur le toit.

4 Marie n' .... pas descendue vite.

5 Mme Lebrun .... allée à la piscine.

6 Vous .... retournés en France?

7 Je ne .... pas parti tôt.

8 Elles .... mortes l'année dernière.

B Make the past participle match the subject of these *être* verbs, by adding agreements (-e, -s, -es) to those that need it.

Example: Mes cousines sont (resté) à l'hôtel. Mes cousines sont resté.*es*... à l'hôtel.

1 Élise est arrivé........ à 11 heures.

2 Jim est mort........ il y a 20 ans.

3 Nous sommes entré........ dans l'épicerie.

4 Marie n'est rentré........ qu'à minuit.

5 Mes stylos ne sont pas tombé........

6 Il est sorti........ avec sa sœur jumelle.

C Complete the sentences.

Example: Je suis allé au collège et elle aussi, elle… ......*est allée au collège.*..........................

1 Tu es monté très vite et les filles aussi, elles ....

2 Les vendeurs sont arrivés et moi aussi, je ....

3 Nous ne sommes pas tombés et eux non plus, ils ....

4 Monsieur Dasse est mort et sa femme aussi, elle ....

D Complete this table to show a reflexive verb in the perfect tense.

je	me	suis	lavé
tu		es	
il			
elle			lavée
nous		sommes	
vous			
ils	se		lavés
elles			

> Reflexive pronouns:
> me   nous
> te   vous
> se   se

E Unjumble these reflexive sentences.

Example: les tard vacances suis Pendant je levée me ....*Pendant les vacances je me suis*........ ......*levée tard.*..

1 sommes Hier tôt soir nous couchés nous ....

2 ne amusés Ils pas parc se bien sont au ....

3 s' collège au Elle ce matin est ennuyée ....

F Form the perfect tense of these reflexive verbs.

Example: Nous (se promener) ......*Nous nous sommes promené(e)s.*..........................

1 Ils (se coucher) ....

2 Elle (s'ennuyer) ....

3 Vous (se disputer) ....

4 Je (s'endormir) ....

The imperfect tense

The imperfect is another tense that you use to talk about the past. You use it to describe what happened over a period of time, what something was like and ongoing actions which were interrupted.

A　Give the imperfect (*je, nous* and *ils* forms) of these verbs.

1 jouer	**je jouais**	**nous jouions**	**ils jouaient**
2 finir	**je finissais**	**nous finissions**	**ils finissaient**
3 perdre	....	....	....
4 avoir	....	....	....
5 être	....	....	....
6 boire	....	....	....
7 aller	....	....	....
8 partir	....	....	....
9 faire	....	....	....
10 lire	....	....	....
11 savoir	....	....	....
12 prendre	....	....	....

B　Change the ending of the imperfect tense to match the new subject.

Example: Il fumait et nous aussi, nous ...... fumions. ....

1 J'attendais et elle aussi, elle ....
2 Vous écriviez et eux aussi, ils ....
3 Tu dormais et le chien aussi, il ....
4 Mes parents regardaient et moi aussi, je ....
5 Mon ami était poli et mes sœurs aussi, elles ....

C　Put the verbs into the imperfect tense, then translate the sentences.

> All verbs except *être* are regular in the imperfect tense.
> **1** Take the *nous* form of the present tense and take off the *-ons* ending: *nous habit(ons)*
> **2** Add the imperfect endings:
> *j'habitais*　　*nous habitions*
> *tu habitais*　　*vous habitiez*
> *il / elle habitait*　*ils / elles habitaient*

Example: Tu ..... visitais .... beaucoup de monuments (visiter)

..... You used to visit lots of monuments. ....

1 Je .... avec mon petit frère sur la plage. (jouer) ....
2 Nous .... très souvent ensemble. (manger) ....
3 Le serveur .... dur pour nous. (travailler) ....
4 On .... beaucoup de glaces. (vendre) ....
5 Papa et Marc .... du ski nautique. (faire) ....
6 Tu .... très content. (être) ....

D　When you are talking or writing about the past, you often need to use a mixture of perfect tense and imperfect tense verbs. Put the following verbs in the correct past tense.

J'[aller] au collège quand j' [voir] l'accident. Il y [avoir] beaucoup de monde. J' [appeler] «au secours!».

....
....
....
....
....

The future tense

> The **near future** is used to say what is going to happen. It is formed using *aller* + infinitive.

A Use the correct part of *aller* to say what you are going to do in the near future and say what these sentences mean.

Example: Je .....*vais*....... regarder un film. ....*I am going to watch a film.*..............................

1 Il .... sortir ce soir. ....

2 Nous .... vendre la maison. ....

3 Vous .... comprendre bientôt. ....

4 Tu .... partir en vacances. ....

5 Maman .... voir un concert. ....

6 Les garçons .... arriver en retard. ....

B Unjumble these sentences in the near future tense.

Example: ta Je à question vais répondre ....*Je vais répondre à ta question.*............................

1 aller allons en Nous ville demain ....

2 partir Quand vas-tu? ....

3 vont leurs Ils devoirs faire ....

4 tennis allez au jouer Vous? ....

5 Lydie cuisine faire la va ....

6 aider Ses vont sœurs ....

> The **future** is used to say what you **will** do. To form the future, add the future endings to the infinitive of the verb: *-ai, -as, -a, -ons, -ez, -ont.*

C Say what everyone will do at the weekend. Put the verb into the future tense.

Example: Je .....*prendrai*..... un bon petit déjeuner. (prendre)

1 Il .... sa nouvelle voiture. (laver)   **5** Elle .... visite à sa tante. (rendre)

2 Tu .... ta copine à manger. (inviter)   **6** Ils .... en France. (arriver)

3 Nous .... nos devoirs. (finir)   **7** Elles .... beaucoup. (bavarder)

4 Vous .... les nouvelles. (attendre)   **8** Je .... une nouvelle robe. (choisir)

D Now try these irregular verbs. Check you know the irregular stem.

Example: vous (pouvoir) .....*vous pourrez*............

1 ils (devoir) ....   **5** tu (avoir) ....

2 nous (savoir) ....   **6** elles (venir) ....

3 je (faire) ....   **7** il (voir) ....

4 elle (être) ....   **8** tu (aller) ....

E Now translate all of exercise D into English.

Example: ....*You will be able to*..............

1 ....   **5** ....

2 ....   **6** ....

3 ....   **7** ....

4 ....   **8** ....

The conditional

The conditional is used to say what you **would** do. It is formed like the future but has different endings. The conditional endings are: -ais, -ais, -ait, -ions, -iez, -aient

A Complete the gaps in this table.

	-er verbs	-ir verbs	-re verbs
	jouer	choisir	vendre
je	jouerais		
tu		choisirais	
Il / elle			vendrait
nous		choisirions	
vous	joueriez		vendriez
Ils / elles		choisiraient	

B What would these people do if they won the lottery? Add the correct part of the verb in brackets and say what the sentence means in English.

Example: Je .....partirais.......... en vacances avec ma famille. (partir)

.....I would go on holiday with my family...

1 Ma mère .... une belle maison. (habiter) ....

2 Vous ne .... plus. (travailler) ....

3 Nous .... beaucoup de pays. (visiter) ....

4 Tu .... de l'argent aux autres. (offrir) ....

5 Ils .... de l'argent à la banque. (mettre) ....

6 Je .... ma vieille voiture. (vendre) ....

Some verbs are irregular in the conditional: *aller: j'irais*   *faire: je ferais*   *voir: je verrais*

C Complete these sentences using the conditional of the verb in brackets. They all have irregular stems, but they keep the same endings as above.

Example: Nous .....ferions.......... une promenade. (faire)

1 Je .... très riche. (être)

2 Vous .... le monde entier. (voir)

3 Ils .... beaucoup d'amis. (avoir)

4 Elle .... épouser son fiancé. (vouloir)

D Write four 'si' sentences of your own, using either the future or conditional tense.

Be careful with 'if' clauses!
- si + present tense + future tense:
  *Si tu **viens**, moi aussi j'**irai**.*
  If you come, I will go too.
- si + imperfect tense + conditional:
  *Si tu **mangeais** correctement, tu n'**aurais** pas faim.*
  If you ate properly, you wouldn't be hungry.

....

....

....

....

....

....

....

The pluperfect tense

> You use the pluperfect to talk about an event which happened one step further back than another past event: 'I **had done** something'.

A Translate these sentences into English.

Example: Si seulement j'avais écouté tes conseils. .....If only I had listened to your advice........

1 Tu avais déjà fini ton déjeuner. ....

2 Nous avions entendu les informations. ....

3 Ils avaient promis de rentrer avant minuit. ....

4 Vous aviez déjà bu toute la bouteille. ....

5 Elle n'avait jamais lu ce livre. ....

6 Ils étaient déjà partis. ....

7 Elle était venue toute seule. ....

8 Les enfants s'étaient couchés de bonne heure. ....

> Like the perfect tense, you form the pluperfect by using an auxiliary (*avoir* or *être*) + a past participle. The difference is that you use the **imperfect tense** of the auxiliary. The verbs which take *être* are the same ones that take *être* in the perfect tense.

B Change these verbs from the perfect into the pluperfect.

Example: J'ai joué   .....J'avais joué........

1 Elle a fini ....   4 Vous (pl) êtes partis ....

2 Nous avons lu ....   5 Tu es tombé? ....

3 Elles sont arrivées ....

C Match the sentence halves, then translate the sentences.

1	J'avais toujours voulu	**a** parti en vacances quand on est arrivé a la maison.
2	Il était	**b** ma voiture dans le parking.
3	Elles étaient	**c** aller à Bordeaux, mais mes parents ont décidé d'aller en Alsace.
4	Heureusement, nous	**d** partie de bonne heure, mais il y avait beaucoup de circulation.
5	Ma sœur était	**e** avions acheté des sandwichs.
6	Mes parents	**f** parties quand il a commencé à pleuvoir.
7	Si tu avais	**g** avaient loué un appartement au bord de la mer.
8	J'avais laissé	**h** gagné le loto, qu'est ce que tu aurais fait?

1 ....

2 ....

3 ....

4 ....

5 ....

6 ....

7 ....

8 ....

Negatives

> You use negatives when you want to say 'not', 'never', 'no longer', 'none', etc. French negatives almost always have two parts: *ne* before the verb and *pas*, etc. after the verb, making a 'sandwich'.

A Match the French to the English translations.

ne … pas	neither … nor
ne … jamais	not any, none
ne … plus	nobody, not anybody
ne … rien	not yet
ne … personne	no longer, no more
ne … aucun	never
ne … que	nothing, not anything
ne … ni … ni…	not
ne … pas encore	only

B Translate these sentences.

Example: Il ne parle pas de son accident. ......He doesn't talk about his accident.......

1 Nous n'aimons ni la géo ni l'histoire. ....

2 Je ne mangerai plus de viande. ....

3 Il n'est jamais arrivé. ....

4 Ils n'ont rien trouvé. ....

5 Je n'envoie aucune carte postale. ....

6 Elle ne fait que deux heures par mois. ....

7 Il ne retournera plus jamais en Italie. ....

C Rearrange the words to make correct sentences.

Example: ne vaisselle fais la Je jamais ....Je ne fais jamais la vaisselle.......

1 aucune Nous idée avons n' ....

2 n'a dix Paul euros que ....

3 fête n' Personne ma venu à est ....

4 bu Ils n'ont café rien au ....

6 achèterez n' de chocolat plus Vous? ....

D Make these sentences negative by inserting the given words. Remember that *du, de la, des, un* and *une* all change to *de (d')* and mean 'any' if they appear after the negative.

Example: Je vois un nuage dans le ciel (ne...pas) ....Je ne vois pas de nuage dans le ciel.......

1 Nous fumerons des cigarettes (ne…plus) ....

2 Elle a dit bonjour (ne…jamais) ....

3 Tu rencontres deux amies en ville (ne…que) ....

4 Il a compris (ne…rien) ....

E Answer these questions in the perfect tense with the negative given.

Example: Il est sorti? (ne...pas) ....Non, il n'est pas sorti.......

1 Ils ont acheté une maison? (ne…jamais) Non, ils ....

2 Elle a fait de la lecture? (ne…pas) ....

3 Elles sont venues? (ne…jamais) ....

Questions

In French you can make something a question by raising your voice at the end of a sentence. However, if you are aiming at a higher grade you need to use question words.

A Make these sentences into questions by using *est-ce que*.

Example: Tu manges des bonbons?   *Est-ce que tu manges des bonbons?*

1 Il peut venir lundi.

2 Vous avez une carte de la ville.

3 Les élèves ont fini leurs devoirs.

4 Elle veut aller en ville.

5 Vous êtes vendeuse.

6 Nous arriverons au collège à l'heure.

B Find the five pairs of questions which mean the same.

1 Est-ce que tu aimes le français?

2 Est-elle française?

3 Est-ce qu'il adore le français?

4 Est-ce que tu as français le mardi?

5 Est-ce qu'il fait du français le mardi?

A Fait-il du français le mardi?

B As-tu français le mardi?

C Aimes-tu le français?

D Est-ce qu'elle est française?

E Adore-t-il le français?

C Separate into ten questions.

Est-cequetuvasenvilledemainmatinest-cequ'iljoueautennisest-cequ'ellepartiraen vacancesenjuilletest-cequetuasperdutaclefest-cequetuasréservéunechambreest-ce quetupréfèresvoyagerenavionouparletrainest-cequelesportablessontutilesest-ceque lechienestmignonest-cequetuveuxalleraucinémaavecmoiest-cequetusaisfairedelavoile

D Match the question word with the rest of the sentence.

1 Qu'

2 Combien de

3 Où

4 Comment

5 Pourquoi

6 À quelle heure

7 Depuis quand

8 Quand

A es-tu venu?

B est-ce que tu aimes faire?

C est-ce que tu vas aider les pauvres?

D habites-tu?

E préférez-vous voyager en France, par le train?

F parles-tu le français?

G est-ce que tu te réveilles le matin?

H personnes habitent à Londres?

E Imagine you get the chance to interview your favourite celebrity. Prepare a list of six questions for them.

Useful little words

A Match up opposite pairs of prepositions.

1	sur	**A**	à la fin
2	devant	**B**	partout
3	loin de	**C**	sans
4	nulle part	**D**	contre
5	pour	**E**	après
6	avec	**F**	sous
7	avant	**G**	derrière
8	au début	**H**	près de

B How many of these prepositions do you recognise? Write the English.

loin de, près de, en face de ....

devant, derrière, à côté ....

nulle part, partout, pour ou contre ....

à droite, à gauche, environ ....

C Fill the gaps with the words in the box. The first letter is given in the text as a clue for some of them. Then translate it into English.

à   À la fin   Après   D'abord   dans   dans   de   et   et   Mais   nulle part
parmi   partout   près de   puis

D ...., je me suis levée à 7 heures, p..................... je me suis lavée. Je suis entrée

d..................... la salle de bains située p..................... ma chambre et j'ai décidé ....prendre

une douche .... me brosser les dents aussi. A..................... ma douche, j'ai

cherché ma serviette p..................... . M..................... je ne l'ai trouvée n..................... .

À .... j'ai réussi .... retrouver ma serviette p..................... mes affaires

.....................je suis rentrée .... ma chambre.

....

....

First of all, I got up at 7 o'clock ....

....

....

....

D All these prepositions have been jumbled up. How quickly can you write them correctly?

1	cnod	**8**	ne eacf ed	**15**	rsev ....
2	etesiun	**9**	zceh		
3	ssaui	**10**	mpria		
4	ttrpuao	**11**	nvdtae		
5	sima	**12**	spèr ed		
6	etdapnn	**13**	oervnni		
7	tvnaa	**14**	ssna		

Useful bits and pieces

A Unjumble these days of the week and seasons.

1 ddvnreei ....
2 ounaetm ....
3 drieecrm ....
4 irvhe ....

5 ildnu ....
6 aeisdm ....
7 mdheican ....
8 téé ....

9 npimetprs ....
10 djuie ....
11 admri ....

B Write out these celebration dates in full.

Example: 15/08: Mon anniversaire = Mon anniversaire, c'est le quinze août.

1 31/12: La Saint-Sylvestre ....
2 08/04: Pâques ....
3 01/01: Le Nouvel An ....
4 14/07: La fête nationale ....

C Write these numbers in words.

(a) 13 ....
(b) 16 ....
(c) 21 ....
(d) 25 ....

(e) 37 ....
(f) 43 ....
(g) 59 ....
(h) 64 ....

(i) 71 ....
(j) 84 ....
(k) 92 ....
(l) 100 ....

D Match the digital times with the correct sentence.

1 02.30
2 11.15
3 01.20
4 3.50
5 11.45
6 08.05

A il est une heure vingt
B il est deux heures et demie
C il est quatre heures moins dix
D il est huit heures cinq
E il est midi moins le quart
F il est onze heures et quart

E Ask for these products using an appropriate quantity from the box.

| un paquet de 4 tranches de cinq livres de un demi kilo de un pot de |
| une bouteille de une boîte de un morceau de une cannette de |

Example: biscuits   Je voudrais .....un paquet de..... biscuits.

1 cerises ....
2 lait ....
3 fromage ....
4 jambon ....
5 sardines ....
6 limonade ....
7 confiture ....
8 pommes de terre ....

Practice Exam Paper: Reading

This Practice Exam Paper has been written to help you practise what you have learned and may not be representative of a real exam paper.

G

1 In town

Read these signs.

A	B	C	D
Camping	**Commissariat**	**Poste**	**Bibliothèque**

E	F	G	H
Château	**Gare**	**Hôtel**	**Syndicat d'initiative**

I	J	K	L
Hôpital	**Boulangerie**	**Boucherie**	**Patinoire**

Which sign goes with which statement? Write the correct letter in each box.

Example: I want to buy a stamp.   C

(a) I want to visit a historic building.   ☐   *(1 mark)*

(b) I want to borrow a book.   ☐   *(1 mark)*

(c) I need to catch a train.   ☐   *(1 mark)*

(d) I would like to report a theft.   ☐   *(1 mark)*

(e) I'd like to buy some bread.   ☐   *(1 mark)*

(f) I need to get some tourist information.   ☐   *(1 mark)*

F

2 The environment

A	B	C	D

E	F	G	H

Read these statements and match each one to a picture. Write the correct letter in each box.

Example: Je vais au collège à vélo.   C

(a) Je recycle le papier.   ☐   *(1 mark)*

(b) Je prends toujours une douche.   ☐   *(1 mark)*

(c) Je protège les animaux.   ☐   *(1 mark)*

(d) Je déteste la pollution.   ☐   *(1 mark)*

3 Amina's school

Read Amina's blog about her school.

> Je m'appelle Amina et j'ai quinze ans. Mon collège est situé dans une petite ville de campagne. J'habite dans un village à dix kilomètres de l'école, alors j'y vais en car.
>
> Au collège, ma matière préférée, c'est le dessin car c'est ma passion, mais par contre, je déteste les sciences car c'est trop difficile. À mon avis, nous avons trop de devoirs, mais en général j'aime bien mon école.

Answer the questions by writing the correct letter in each box.

Example: How old is Amina?

A	14
B	15
C	16

B

(a) Where is Amina's school?

A	in a village
B	in a small town
C	in the mountains

(1 mark)

(b) How does she get to school?

A	by coach
B	by car
C	by train

(1 mark)

(c) What is her favourite subject?

A	science
B	design and technology
C	art

(1 mark)

(d) What reason does she give for hating a subject?

A	it's hard
B	it's boring
C	she dislikes the teacher

(1 mark)

(e) What does she object to?

A	the teachers
B	too much homework
C	getting too tired

(1 mark)

4 Lifestyles

Read what these young people say about their lifestyles.

> **Océane:** Je vais au centre de sport tous les jours. Je suis contente car je suis en forme mais je n'ai pas le temps de rencontrer mes amies.
>
> **Carole:** Je suis membre d'un club de natation. Je me suis faite de nouveaux amis, mais je suis souvent fatiguée le soir.
>
> **Delphine:** Je ne mange plus de chocolat. Je n'ai plus mal aux dents mais j'ai commencé à fumer!

Give an advantage and a disadvantage of each person's lifestyle **in English**.

	Advantage	Disadvantage	
Example: Océane	she is fit	no time to meet friends	
Carole			(2 marks)
Delphine			(2 marks)

5 Free time activities

Read what these three people say about their hobbies.

> **Benjamin**: J'adore tous les sports sauf le ski. Je joue dans une équipe de volley le samedi et je nage à la piscine trois fois par semaine. Le weekend dernier, j'ai fait de la planche à voile avec mon oncle sur un lac qui se trouve tout près de chez nous.
>
> **Lionel**: Moi, je ne suis pas sportif mais j'aime les sports d'hiver et la semaine dernière j'ai fait du ski dans les Alpes avec quelques copains. J'adore la lecture et j'écoute de la musique tous les jours dans ma chambre. Je voudrais bien acheter un nouvel ordinateur mais je n'ai pas assez d'argent.
>
> **Quentin**: Je ne peux pas vivre sans mon portable car j'adore rester en contact avec mes amis et j'aime aussi surfer sur Internet. Je suis assez sportif aussi. Je fais beaucoup de cyclisme et de cheval. Récemment, je suis allé à la patinoire avec un groupe de copains et on s'est bien amusés.

Answer these questions. Write **B** (Benjamin), **L** (Lionel) or **Q** (Quentin) in each box.

Example: Who is not sporty?   L

(a) Who likes skiing?		*(1 mark)*
(b) Who loves his mobile?		*(1 mark)*
(c) Who recently went windsurfing?		*(1 mark)*
(d) Who regularly plays a team sport?		*(1 mark)*
(e) Who goes horse riding?		*(1 mark)*
(f) Who is short of money?		*(1 mark)*
(g) Who likes reading?		*(1 mark)*

6 Holidays

Read Marcel's account of his holiday.

> Je viens de rentrer de vacances en Belgique avec ma famille. Nous y avons passé deux semaines dans un grand hôtel au bord de la mer, ce qui m'a plu car j'adore les vues nautiques. Ma chambre était spacieuse et j'aimais ça, pourtant il n'y avait pas assez d'eau chaude le matin, ce qui m'a embêté.
>
> Les repas au restaurant au rez-de-chaussée étaient vraiment délicieux, mais le service était un peu lent et à mon avis, les serveurs n'étaient pas polis.
>
> Il y avait une piscine en plein air où j'ai nagé tous les soirs et c'était marrant. Nous avons fait une excursion dans une ville voisine où je me suis bien amusé dans un petit parc d'attractions. On a aussi visité un musée, ce que j'ai trouvé ennuyeux.
>
> Le vol de retour était nul car on a dû attendre six heures à l'aéroport et mon père a perdu ses lunettes de soleil.

What is Marcel's opinion of each of the following? Write **P** (positive), **N** (negative) or **P/N** (both positive and negative) in each box.

Example: The location of the hotel   P

(a) Marcel's room ___ *(1 mark)*

(b) The meals in the restaurant ___ *(1 mark)*

(c) The service in the restaurant ___ *(1 mark)*

(d) The swimming pool ___ *(1 mark)*

(e) The trip to a nearby town ___ *(1 mark)*

(f) The journey home ___ *(1 mark)*

7 Home life

Read Caroline's account of her home life.

> J'habite une grande maison individuelle dans la banlieue de Marseille avec mes parents, ma sœur et notre chien. Chez nous, c'est mon père qui fait le jardinage mais je partage la cuisine avec ma mère. Ma sœur, qui est très paresseuse, ne fait rien à la maison normalement, mais elle promène le chien de temps en temps le weekend. Pendant la semaine, mon père le promène avant d'aller au travail.
>
> La semaine dernière, c'était l'anniversaire de ma tante et on a organisé une fête pour elle chez nous. J'ai nettoyé le salon le matin pendant que mes parents faisaient les courses. Même ma sœur a aidé un peu parce qu'elle a rangé la cave. Il y avait beaucoup d'invités et tout le monde s'est bien amusé.
>
> Demain, je vais ranger ma chambre et celle de ma sœur car ma cousine va passer quelques jours chez nous.

Which of these statements are true? Write the correct **five** letters in the boxes.

A	Caroline has one sister.
B	Caroline lives in a semi-detached house.
C	She lives in the centre of Marseille.
D	Her dad works in the garden.
E	Her mum does all the cooking.
F	Her sister usually does nothing to help at home.
G	Her dad always walks the dog.
H	Last week there was a party at Caroline's house.
I	Caroline's parents did the shopping.
J	Caroline's sister did some tidying up.
K	It was a small party.
L	Caroline's cousin will tidy the bedrooms.

Example: [A]

[ ] *(1 mark)* [ ] *(1 mark)* [ ] *(1 mark)* [ ] *(1 mark)* [ ] *(1 mark)*

8 Life in a French-speaking country

Read Mohammed's email about life in Mali.

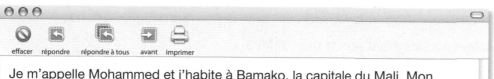

> Je m'appelle Mohammed et j'habite à Bamako, la capitale du Mali. Mon pays est assez pauvre et il y plein de problèmes ici dont le chômage est le plus grave. Mon père est sans emploi depuis plus de dix ans et moi-même j'ai peur de ne pas trouver de travail à l'avenir.
>
> Ma ville est dans le sud du pays et il y fait très chaud toute l'année, mais dans le nord du pays il ne pleut presque jamais et on ne peut pas cultiver assez de nourriture, alors on a besoin d'aide. Mon collège est énorme et il y a cinquante élèves dans ma classe de français. On commence tôt pour éviter la chaleur de la journée et les salles ne sont pas bien équipées. Heureusement, nous venons de recevoir du matériel scolaire d'une association caritative, ce qui m'a permis de pouvoir faire des recherches à l'aide d'un ordinateur.
>
> On fabrique beaucoup de coton ici mais je ne voudrais pas travailler dans les champs avec ceux qui ont l'occasion de trouver un emploi. Je travaille dur à l'école parce que j'aimerais être médecin un jour.

Answer these questions **in English**.

Example: Where does Mohammed live? in Bamako

(a) What is the most serious problem facing Mali, according to Mohammed?

.... *(1 mark)*

(b) What exactly does Mohammed tell us about his dad? What are Mohammed's fears for the future?

(i) ....

(ii) .... *(2 marks)*

(c) What can the people in the north of Mali not do well?

.... *(1 mark)*

(d) Why do lessons start early in Mohammed's school?

.... *(1 mark)*

(e) What has just happened in Mohammed's school? Why do you think he is pleased as a result?

(i) ....

(ii) .... *(2 marks)*

(f) What would Mohammed like to do in the future?

.... *(1 mark)*

9 New technologies

Read these sentences about new technologies.

Choose a word from the grid to fill each gap. Write the correct letter in each box.

Example: Mes parents m'ont acheté un ⬚B MP3.

(a) Je trouve Internet super si on veut chercher des ⬚ quand on fait les devoirs. *(1 mark)*

(b) Je ⬚ d'acheter un nouvel ordinateur. *(1 mark)*

(c) Je reste en contact avec mes cousins au Maroc. Je leur ⬚ des e-mails tous les jours. *(1 mark)*

(d) Mon portable est indispensable car je ⬚ environ cinq textos par heure. *(1 mark)*

(e) Avec la télé par satellite, on ⬚ regarder un grand nombre d'émissions
et j'aime le choix. *(1 mark)*

(f) Mon portable est vraiment ⬚ si on veut prendre des photos. *(1 mark)*

(g) Un inconvénient de la technologie, c'est qu'on peut passer ⬚ de temps devant
un écran. *(1 mark)*

(h) Je voudrais ⬚ aux forums dans le futur parce que ça me semble très intéressant. *(1 mark)*

A	renseignements
B	lecteur
C	peut
D	acheter
E	envoie
F	reçois
G	shopping
H	participer
I	utile
J	forums
K	trop
L	viens

Practice Exam Paper: Listening

This Practice Exam Paper has been written to help you practise what you have learned and may not be representative of a real exam paper.

1 Personal information

Listen to these young people talking about themselves. Fill in the gaps **in English**.

Example: I have ....green.............................. eyes.

1 I have short ....hair. *(1 mark)*

2 I am quite .... *(1 mark)*

3 I have .... eyes. *(1 mark)*

4 People say that I am .... *(1 mark)*

5 In my opinion I am rather .... *(1 mark)*

6 My favourite colour is .... *(1 mark)*

2 Leisure activities

A B C D

E F G H

What are these people talking about? Choose a picture to go with each person. Write the correct letter in each box.

Example: G

1 ☐ *(1 mark)*

2 ☐ *(1 mark)*

3 ☐ *(1 mark)*

4 ☐ *(1 mark)*

3 Holidays and holiday activities

Listen to these people talking about their holidays. Which **destination** and which **activity** does each person mention? Write the correct letters and numbers in the boxes.

Destinations:

A	mountains
B	countryside
C	seaside
D	lake
E	town centre
F	theme park

Activities:

1	sailing
2	water skiing
3	buying ice creams
4	sunbathing
5	fishing
6	walking

	Destination	**Activity**	
Example:	F	3	
1			*(2 marks)*
2			*(2 marks)*
3			*(2 marks)*

4 Jobs

Listen to these young people talking about their jobs. Give an advantage and a disadvantage of each job **in English**.

	Advantage	**Disadvantage**	
Example:	easy	not enough holidays	
1			*(2 marks)*
2			*(2 marks)*
3			*(2 marks)*

5 School

Listen to Marthe talking about her school.

What are her opinions of the following? Write **P** (positive), **N** (negative) or **P/N** (both positive and negative) in each box.

Example: School buildings   N

1	Teachers		*(1 mark)*
2	Canteen		*(1 mark)*
3	School rules		*(1 mark)*
4	English		*(1 mark)*
5	Homework		*(1 mark)*

6 Lifestyles

Listen to these young people talking about stress in their lives.

What **two** things does each person do to cope with stress? Write the correct letters in the boxes.

A	watch television	F	read
B	listen to music	G	go out with friends
C	eat chocolate	H	go to sleep
D	go to the doctor's	I	have a hot drink
E	do physical activity	J	talk to sisters

Example: Guillaume `C` `J`

1 Lise ☐ ☐ *(2 marks)*

2 Anya ☐ ☐ *(2 marks)*

3 Hugo ☐ ☐ *(2 marks)*

7 Where I live

Listen to Serge talking about where he lives.

Choose the correct ending for each sentence. Write the correct letter in each box.

Example: Serge lives in the …

A	north.
B	south.
C	east.

`B`

Part 1

1 According to Serge, the best thing about his town is …

A	the harbour.
B	the shops.
C	the sports facilities.

☐ *(1 mark)*

2 In his opinion, the worst thing about his town is …

A	the weather.
B	the sports facilities.
C	the traffic.

☐ *(1 mark)*

Part 2

3 Yesterday Serge decided to …

A	plan his summer holiday.
B	become a volunteer.
C	organise a party.

☐ *(1 mark)*

4 He hopes to …

A	move to a different town.
B	go skiing.
C	enjoy a festival.

☐ *(1 mark)*

8 **The environment**

Listen to the passage, then answer the questions **in English**.

Part 1

(a) What percentage of French people used to travel by bus in 2000? .... *(1 mark)*

(b) Why are more people using the bus? Give **two** reasons.

(i) ....

(ii) .... *(2 marks)*

Part 2

(c) What does Julien say we should do less? .... *(1 mark)*

(d) What **three** things has Julien done in the past to help the environment?

(i) ....

(ii) ....

(iii) .... *(3 marks)*

Part 3

(e) Why have some people in his town annoyed him?

.... *(1 mark)*

(f) What example does he give to demonstrate this problem?

.... *(1 mark)*

9 **Future plans**

Part 1

Listen to Randha talking about her future. Which of these statements are true? Write the correct **three** letters in the boxes.

A	Randha was born in France.	E	Her grandparents would like to live with her family.
B	Randha lives in Rouen.	F	Her parents live in Africa.
C	She does not want to go to university.	G	Randha cannot find a job.
D	She would like to continue her education.	H	Randha needs to earn some money to help her family.

B

☐ *(1 mark)* ☐ *(1 mark)* ☐ *(1 mark)*

Part 2

Now listen to Corinne talking about her future. Which of these statements are true? Write the correct **three** letters in the boxes.

A	Corinne would like to be a model.	D	Corinne wants to find a job quickly.
B	She used to work as a model.	E	She will soon take her exams.
C	Corinne thinks she can persuade her mum to agree to her plans.	F	She would like a job in IT.

☐ *(1 mark)* ☐ *(1 mark)* ☐ *(1 mark)*

Answers

Lifestyle

1. Birthdays
1 B, D, E, G, I *(in any order)*

2 **(a)** VIGNAU *(must be completely correct)*

(b) 21st June *(must be completely correct)*

(c) Scotland

(d) shopping

(e) ice skating

(f) sailing

2. Pets
3 **(a)** E **(b)** B **(c)** C **(d)** F

4 **1** P **2** N **3** P/N **4** N

3. Physical description
5 **(a)** B **(b)** A **(c)** E **(d)** C

6 **1** B **2** F **3** E **4** D

4. Personality
7 A, B, D, I *(in any order)*

8 **(a)** F **(b)** C **(c)** D **(d)** B

5. Brothers and sisters
9 **(a)** T **(b)** F **(c)** ? **(d)** ?
(e) T **(f)** ?

10 **(a)** C **(b)** A **(c)** F **(d)** B

6. Family
11 A, E, G, I, K *(in any order)*

12 **(a)** 13

(b) **(i)** Swiss **(ii)** same age as mother *(2)*

(c) would not / did not obey / was disobedient *OR* would not / did not talk to them

(d) nearby *OR* near their house *OR* not far away

(e) (they) allow him to go out late (sometimes)

(f) (he thinks) he is lucky *(1)* because they / all his parents / all three love him *(1)*

7. Friends
13 **(a)** Carla **(b)** Suzanne **(c)** Maryse
(d) Lola

14 **1** A **2** D **3** F **4** C

8. Daily routine
15 **(a)** shower **(b)** kitchen **(c)** 8.15
(d) on foot

16 **Frank:** Advantage: can chat to family *(1)*
Disadvantage: cannot watch TV *(1)*

Mélissa: Advantage: can relax *(1)*
Disadvantage: very tired *(1)*

9. Breakfast
17 **(a)** T **(b)** F **(c)** F **(d)** T
(e) ? **(f)** T

18 **(a)** C **(b)** B **(c)** A **(d)** A

10. Eating at home
19 **(a)** one month ago

(b) **(i)** could be stressful
(ii) still had a cold *(2)*

(c) **(i)** show cooking skills
(ii) mother could relax *(2)*

(d) she disliked everything

(e) **(i)** grateful
(ii) found it unbelievable *(2)*

20 **(a)** pasta **(b)** vegetables **(c)** steak
(d) cheese

11. Eating in a café
21 **(a)** G **(b)** I **(c)** F **(d)** B
(e) D **(f)** K **(g)** N **(h)** P

22 **1** N **2** P **3** P/N **4** P

12. Eating in a restaurant
23 **(a)** A **(b)** N **(c)** C **(d)** N
(e) N **(f)** C **(g)** A **(h)** A

24 **1** chicken / vegetables *(2)*
2 fruit / meat *(2)*
3 pork / fish *(2)*
4 strawberries / bananas *(2)*

13. Healthy eating
25 **(a)** Roger **(b)** Ibrahim **(c)** Pauline
(d) Robert

26 **(a)** E **(b)** G **(c)** I **(d)** C

14. Health issues
27 **(a)** in too much of a hurry

(b) **(i)** salads *(1)* and **(ii)** light meals *(1)* are on offer in the work canteen

(c) a friend / doctor said it wasn't recommended

(d) bad for her teeth

(e) might put on weight

(f) might be annoyed

28 C, E, F, I *(in any order)*

15. Health problems
29 **(b)** C **(c)** B **(d)** F **(e)** A **(f)** D

30 **(a)** to be **(i)** sociable and **(ii)** chatty *(2)*

(b) **(i)** to forget her school problems **(ii)** not drinking alcohol *(2)*

(c) *any three of:* road accidents / violence / serious illnesses / effects on others *(3)*

16. Relationship plans
31 (a) N **(b)** L **(c)** A **(d)** L
(e) L **(f)** N

32 1 kind / appearance *(2)*
2 funny / money *(2)*
3 sporty / family *(2)*
4 quiet *OR* calm / smokes *(2)*

17. Social issues
33 (a) B **(b)** C **(c)** B **(d)** A **(e)** B

34 1 H **2** E **3** F **4** B

18. Social problems
35 (b) H **(c)** E **(d)** D **(e)** B **(f)** F

36 (a) she's dead **(b)** lack of money

(c) found a job **(d)** gave computers to
school **(e)** rich countries should help

Leisure

19. Hobbies
1 (a) D **(b)** A **(c)** F **(d)** B
(e) I **(f)** E **(g)** H **(h)** J

2 1 D **2** F **3** C **4** A

20. Sport
3 (a) B **(b)** C **(c)** A **(d)** B

4 1 A **2** F **3** D **4** B

21. Going out
5 A, B, E, G, H *(in any order)*

6 1 C **2** A **3** D **4** F

22. Last weekend
7 (a) L **(b)** Z **(c)** A **(d)** Z

8 (a) B **(b)** J **(c)** C **(d)** B

23. Television
9 (a) B **(b)** I **(c)** A **(d)** D
(e) G **(f)** E

10 1 N **2** P **3** P/N **4** N
5 N **6** P/N

24. Cinema
11 (a) everyone **(b)** high demand

(c) (i) be seated before start of film
(ii) turn off mobile phone *(2)*

(d) (i) they get tired
(ii) they lose concentration *(2)*

(e) (i) free **(ii)** safe *(2)*

12 (a) C **(b)** C **(c)** A **(d)** B

25. Music
13 (a) T **(b)** T **(c)** F **(d)** ?
(e) T **(f)** F

14 1 A **2** G **3** D **4** B

26. New technology
15 B, C, F, H *(in any order)*

16 1 take photos **2** send texts
3 store music **4** chat with my friends

27. Internet language
17 A, C, F, G *(in any order)*

18 1 A **2** B **3** E **4** F

28. Internet pros and cons
19 (a) F **(b)** ? **(c)** F **(d)** T
(e) T **(f)** F

20 1 F **2** B **3** C **4** E

29. Shops
21 (a) E **(b)** I **(c)** C **(d)** G
(e) J **(f)** A

22 1 clothes shop / dress *(2)*
2 fish shop / salmon *(2)*
3 post office / stamps *(2)*

30. Food shopping
23 (a) D **(b)** H **(c)** C **(d)** G
(e) A **(f)** L

24 B, D, E, G, K, M *(in any order)*

31. Shopping
25 (a) F **(b)** T **(c)** F **(d)** ?
(e) T **(f)** F **(g)** F **(h)** F

26 1 C **2** B **3** A **4** D

32. Clothes
27 (a) D **(b)** A **(c)** E **(d)** C

28 (a) B **(b)** C **(c)** B **(d)** A

33. Clothes shopping
29 (a) (i) shops too busy
(ii) not enough staff *(2)*

(b) salespeople have more time to help

(c) (winter) (over)coat

(d) only had small and large sizes left

(e) (i) had been saving for two months
(ii) hadn't bought herself anything for a
long time *(2)*

(f) good taste (in clothes)

30 C, D, G, H *(in any order)*

34. Returning items
31 1 D **2** F **3** E **4** A
5 H **6** J **7** L **8** O

32 (a) small **(b)** awful **(c)** 17 **(d)** 50

35. Shopping preferences
33 (a) Madeleine **(b)** Luc **(c)** Jeannot
(d) Aline **(e)** Nadège **(f)** Pierrot

34 Mimi: F, C *(2)*, Janina: A, E *(2)*

36. Pocket money
35 (a) G **(b)** E **(c)** C **(d)** A

36 (a) A **(b)** A **(c)** C **(d)** B

37. Holiday destinations
37 C, D, G, H *(in any order)*

38 1 P/N **2** N **3** P **4** N

38. Holiday accommodation
39 (a) C (b) A (c) H (d) D
(e) B (f) G

40 1 N 2 S 3 U 4 N
(v) S

39. Booking accommodation
41 (a) they had a nice holiday there last year

(b) to get the best rooms

(c) overlooking the pool

(d) staying indoors

(e) a week

(f) (i) children tire easily (ii) children argue *(2)*

(g) relaxing

42 1 double 2 balcony
3 single 4 3 nights

40. Staying in a hotel
43 (a) E (b) D (c) F (d) A

44 (a) (i) it overlooks a lake (ii) windsurfing *(2)*

(b) (i) air conditioning (in all rooms)
(ii) rooms on ground floor *(2)*

(c) (i) brother lost his key (ii) it rained *(2)*

41. Camping
45 (a) M (b) T (c) C (d) T
(e) M (f) M

46 ☺ B, G *(in any order)* ☹ E, F *(in any order)*

42. Holiday activities
47 B, C, F, H *(in any order)*

48 (a) B (b) C (c) C (d) A (e) A

43. Holiday preferences
49 (a) F (b) ? (c) T (d) T
(e) F (f) F (g) T (h) ?

50 1 A 2 F 3 H 4 B

44. Holiday plans
51 (a) his dad won't be there to (i) pay for everything (ii) sort out problems *(2)*

(b) (i) more freedom (ii) stay out late(r) *(2)*

(c) not busy

(d) go to nightclubs

(e) (i) reasonable price (ii) games room *(2)*

52 (a) H (b) A (c) E (d) F

45. Holiday experiences
53 B, E, G, H *(in any order)*

54 (a) J (b) L (c) L/J (d) J
(e) L/J (f) J

Home and environment

46. Countries
1 (a) J (b) F (c) K (d) M
(e) D (f) B (g) N (h) H

2 1 G 2 E 3 B 4 H
5 F

47. My house
3 (a) P/N (b) P (c) N (d) P
(e) N (f) P/N

4 1 G 2 H 3 D 4 B

48. My room
5 (a) ? (b) F (c) T (d) F
(e) F (f) ? (g) T (h) T

6 (a) Advantage: can chat until late (1)
Disadvantage: brother never makes his bed (1)

(b) Advantage: can play loud music (1)
Disadvantage: bathroom too far away (1)

49. Helping at home
7 (a) A (b) E (c) H (d) G
(e) D (f) C (g) J (h) L

8 1 P/N 2 P 3 P/N 4 P
5 N 6 N

50. Where I live
9 (a) (i) on 10th floor of block of council flats
(ii) in poor area of Paris *(2)*

(b) (i) bad condition (ii) lift not working *(2)*

(c) only 3 bedrooms for mother, father and 6 children

(d) *any two of:* close to factory / polluted atmosphere / noisy / risk of being attacked *(2)*

(e) (i) was chased by gang of youths
(ii) dropped / lost his mobile *(2)*

(f) build youth club OR sports centre

10 D, E, H, I *(in any order)*

51. Places in town
11 (a) 110 (b) 3 km (c) no smoking
(d) Sunday

12 (a) C (b) C (c) B (d) A

52. Things to do in town
13 (a) ? (b) T (c) F (d) T
(e) T (f) ? (g) T

14 B, C, E, J, K *(in any order)*

53. Tourist attractions
15 (a) C (b) B (c) E (d) I
(e) D (f) L (g) F

16 1 went to see a show
2 go to shopping centre
3 (a) police station (b) lost purse *(2)*
4 going to tourist attractions

54. Signs around town
17 (a) D (b) I (c) A (d) G

18 1 F 2 A 3 E 4 C

55. Opinions of where you live
19 (a) Z (b) L (c) L (d) D

20 **1** Advantage: I *(1)* / Disadvantage: H *(1)*
2 Advantage: A *(1)* / Disadvantage: C *(1)*
3 Advantage: E *(1)* / Disadvantage: D *(1)*

56. Town description

21 **(a)** 18 months

(b) *any two of:* too crowded / lots of factories / dirty *(2)*

(c) never any traffic jams

(d) to do water sports

(e) watch birds / see wild flowers *(2)*

(f) an ice rink will be built

22 **1** H   **2** B   **3** D   **4** A

57. Weather

23 **(a)** D   **(b)** G   **(c)** E   **(d)** F   **(e)** C

24 **(a)** snowing   **(b)** sunny
(c) windy   **(d)** raining

58. Celebrations at home

25 **(a)** K   **(b)** L   **(c)** J   **(d)** J
(e) K   **(f)** K

26 **1** E   **2** C   **3** A   **4** D

59. Directions

27 C, D, F, H *(in any order)*

28 **1** E   **2** A   **3** D   **4** C

60. At the railway station

29 **(a)** A   **(b)** E   **(c)** G   **(d)** F
(e) I   **(f)** C   **(g)** B   **(h)** J

30 **(i)** D   **(ii)** C   **(iii)** E   **(iv)** F

61. Travelling

31 **(a)** F   **(b)** A   **(c)** G   **(d)** H

32 **(a)** F   **(b)** C   **(c)** A   **(d)** B

62. Transport

33 **(a)** Oscar   **(b)** Tamsir
(c) Hugo   **(d)** Laure

34 **(i)** **(a)** before 1940 **(b)** roads built / cheaper to build roads than to put down tram rails *(2)* **(c)** they disappeared

(ii) **(a)** price of petrol / pollution from cars *(2)* **(b)** shared by pedestrians, bikes and vehicles **(c)** at least 21

63. The environment

35 **(a)** G   **(b)** F   **(c)** K   **(d)** I
(e) D   **(f)** J   **(g)** L   **(h)** A

36 B, C, E, G *(in any order)*

64. Environmental problems

37 **(a)** T   **(b)** ?   **(c)** F   **(d)** T
(e) F   **(f)** F   **(g)** T   **(h)** ?

38 **(i)** C   **(ii)** E   **(iii)** D   **(iv)** G

65. What I do to be 'green'

39 **(a)** M   **(b)** Y   **(c)** D
(d) M   **(e)** D   **(f)** Y

40 **1** B   **2** D   **3** H   **4** E

66. News headlines

41 **(a)** E   **(b)** A   **(c)** D   **(d)** C

42 **1** C   **2** A   **3** C   **4** B

Work and education

67. School subjects

1 **(a)** G   **(b)** B   **(c)** I   **(d)** H

2 B, D, G, H, J *(in any order)*

68. Opinions of school

3 **(a)** L   **(b)** N   **(c)** E   **(d)** D
(e) I   **(f)** J   **(g)** F   **(h)** O

4 **1** P   **2** P/N   **3** P   **4** N
5 P/N   **6** N

69. School routine

5 **(a)** T   **(b)** J   **(c)** M   **(d)** J
(e) T   **(f)** M

6 **1** 4 p.m.   **2** chats to friends
3 an hour   **4** playground / yard

70. Comparing schools

7 C, E, F, I *(in any order)*

8 A, D, H, I *(in any order)*

71. Primary school

9 **(a)** E   **(b)** A   **(c)** B   **(d)** F   **(e)** K

10 **1** B   **2** A   **3** B   **4** C

72. Rules at school

11 **(a)** E   **(b)** A   **(c)** F   **(d)** I   **(e)** B

12 **1** turn off mobiles
2 she got a detention
3 in a PE lesson
4 running in the corridors
5 not being allowed to talk in the library
6 not many books OR no one reads in the library OR should be allowed to talk quietly when using the computers
7 no swearing / it's impolite (2)

73. Problems at school

13 **(a)** E   **(b)** D   **(c)** I   **(d)** G   **(e)** B

14 **1** discuss problems with parents
2 try to make new friends
3 speak to science teacher
4 do more homework
5 be more confident

74. Future education

15 **(a)** F   **(b)** ?   **(c)** F   **(d)** T
(e) F   **(f)** ?

16 B, C, D, G *(in any order)*

75. Future plans

17 **(a)** H   **(b)** J   **(c)** N   **(d)** K
(e) E   **(f)** L   **(g)** B   **(h)** A

18 **1** D   **2** B   **3** A   **4** C
5 F   **6** H

76. Jobs

19 **(a)** H **(b)** C **(c)** G **(d)** F

20 **1** a postman **2** a builder
3 an actress **4** a housewife
5 a plumber **6** an accountant

77. Job adverts

21 A, C, F, G *(in any order)*

22 **1** C **2** C **3** A **4** B

78. CV

23 B, E, G, H, I *(in any order)*

24 Age: 16, School subject: art, Sport: volleyball, Hobby: cinema

79. Job application

25 **(a)** F **(b)** T **(c)** T **(d)** ?
(e) F **(f)** T **(g)** ? **(h)** T

26 **1** travel agency
2 has worked in tourist office
3 in a bookshop
4 **(a)** hard-working **(b)** responsible *(2)*
5 16th January
6 the day after tomorrow

80. Job interview

27 **1** helping a childminder
2 primary school teacher
3 went shopping
4 15 minutes
5 *any two of:* babysitting / good at French / did a course *(2)*
6 about salary and working hours

28 **1** very hardworking
2 chemistry
3 clothes shop
4 honest

81. Opinions about jobs

29 **(a)** Advantage: responsible job *(1)*
Disadvantage: hours too long *(1)*

(b) Advantage: travel lots *(1)*
Disadvantage: always standing *(1)*

(c) Advantage: easy *(1)*
Disadvantage: boring *(1)*

30 **1** G / K *(2)* **2** D / O *(2)* **3** F / N *(2)*

82. Part-time work

31 A, D, F, H, J *(in any order)*

32 **1** C **2** D **3** A **4** E

83. Work experience

33 **(a)** F **(b)** T **(c)** ?
(d) T **(e)** F **(f)** F

34 **1** H **2** G **3** E **4** C

84. My work experience

35 **(a)** F **(b)** E **(c)** H
(d) A **(e)** B **(f)** C **(g)** I

36 **1** N **2** P/N **3** N
4 P **5** P/N **6** N **7** P

Grammar

85. Articles 1

A **1** les commerces **2** la pharmacie
3 les toilettes **4** l'hôtel
5 les cinémas **6** le bowling
7 la gare **8** le parking
9 les rues **10** l'appartement

B **1** la chienne **2** les serpents
3 l'araignée **4** le chat
5 la tortue **6** l'éléphant
7 les poissons **8** le canard
9 la mouche **10** les cochons d'Inde
11 la grenouille **12** le singe

C **1** un salon **2** une salle de bains
3 un jardin **4** une chambre
5 un sous-sol **6** une cuisine
7 une salle à manger

D *le chien* – les chiens, un château – *des châteaux,* l'animal – *les animaux, une voiture* – des voitures

le nez – *les nez,* le bateau – *les bateaux,* un hôtel – *des hôtels,* l'arbre – les arbres

une page – des pages, *l'eau* – les eaux, une araignée – *des araignées*

la destination – les destinations

86. Articles 2

A **1** des œufs **2** de la confiture
3 du pain **4** des haricots verts
5 de l'eau minérale **6** du jambon
7 des frites **8** de la crème
9 de l'huile **10** du riz

B Tu veux DES pâtes, des abricots, du fromage, du chocolat, des olives, du porc, des pommes de terre, du ketchup, de l'ananas, du potage, des oeufs, du sel et du poivre?

C **1** Je n'ai pas d'argent. I don't have any money.
2 Je n'ai pas de pain. I don't have any bread.
3 Je n'ai pas de céréales. I don't have any cereals.
4 Je n'ai pas de pizza. I don't have any pizza.

D Tu as des fruits et des légumes? Oui, j'ai des fruits mais je n'ai pas de légumes. Par exemple, j'ai des pêches et des cerises mais je n'ai pas de carottes ni de pommes de terre. Cependant, j'ai du pain et du nutella, donc on peut manger des sandwichs.

E **1** à la patinoire **2** à la crêperie
3 au théâtre **4** à l'hôtel de ville
5 aux magasins **6** au café-tabac

F **1** au salon **2** à la cuisine
3 à la salle de bains **4** aux chambres
5 à la salle de jeux **6** au jardin
7 à l'atelier **8** au grenier
9 à la cave **10** à l'entrée
11 au garage **12** à la salle à manger

87. Adjectives

A 1 Ma mère est petite.
   2 Mon père est grand.
   3 Ma maison est belle.
   4 Mon chat est noir.
   5 Elle est heureuse.
   6 Les fenêtres sont chères.

B 1 Mon chien est triste.
   2 Mes crayons sont blancs.
   3 Ma mère est intelligente.
   4 Mes frères sont timides.
   5 Mes sœurs sont grosses.
   6 Ma chatte est très mignonne.

C

grand	grande	**grands**	grandes	big/tall
petit	petite	**petits**	**petites**	**small**
noir	**noire**	noirs	**noires**	**black**
neuf	neuve	**neufs**	neuves	**new**
dernier	**dernière**	derniers	**dernières**	last
marron	**marron**	marron	**marron**	(chestnut) **brown**
triste	**triste**	tristes	**tristes**	sad
sérieux	**sérieuse**	sérieux	**sérieuses**	**serious**
gentil	gentille	**gentils**	gentilles	kind
sec	sèche	secs	**sèches**	**dry**
drôle	**drôle**	drôles	**drôles**	funny
vieux	vieille	**vieux**	vieilles	old
beau	belle	beaux	**belles**	**beautiful**
ancien	**ancienne**	anciens	**anciennes**	ancient
blanc	**blanche**	blancs	**blanches**	white
sportif	sportive	**sportifs**	sportives	**sporty**

D 1 Elle a de beaux yeux bleus.
   2 Les meilleures fleurs jaunes
   3 Mes vieux baskets blancs
   4 Mes pauvres parents malades

88. Possessives

A 1 Dans MA famille, il y a mon père, ma mère, ma sœur et mes deux frères. Ma grand-mère vient souvent nous rendre visite avec mon grand-père. Mon amie adore mes grands-parents et elle vient jouer avec toutes mes affaires quand ils sont là.
   2 Dans SA chambre, elle a son lit, ses livres, son bureau, sa télévision, ses bijoux, son téléphone et son nounours.
   3 Dans NOTRE collège, nous avons nos professeurs, notre bibliothèque, notre cantine et notre terrain de sport. Et vous, qu'est-ce que vous avez dans votre collège et dans vos salles de classe? Vous avez vos tableaux blancs interactifs et votre gymnase?

4 **(a)** Comment s'appellent ton père et ta mère?
   (b) Qu'est-ce que tu achètes avec ton argent?
   (c) C'est quand ton anniversaire?
   (d) Qu'est-ce qu'il y a dans ta ville ou ton village?
5 Dans LEUR village, ils ont leur mairie, leurs cinémas, leur pharmacie, leur boulangerie, leurs cafés, leurs parcs, leur hôpital, leur école, tous leurs petits commerces.

B *Examples from the table:* Mon fromage est très timide, Nos copines ne sont pas très honnêtes, Leurs photos sont assez jaunes, Vos gâteaux sont très romantiques!

C 1 Les pulls? Ce sont les miens!
   2 Les jupes? Ce sont les miennes!
   3 Le jogging? C'est le mien!

89. Comparisons

A Lydie est la plus intelligente. Paul est le moins intelligent.

B *Other examples:* Anna est pire en français qu'Antoine. Anna est la meilleure en dessin.

C 1 Philippe est aussi grand que Sara. = Philippe is as tall as Sara.
   2 Les maths sont plus difficiles que la musique. = Maths is more difficult than music.
   3 Les bonbons sont moins sains que les fruits. = Sweets are not as healthy as fruit.
   4 Une cravate est moins confortable qu'un jogging. = A tie is less comfortable than a tracksuit.
   5 La chimie est aussi intéressante que l'anglais. = Chemistry is as interesting as English.

D 1 Les kiwis sont les fruits les plus sains.
   2 L'hiver est la saison la plus froide.
   3 Londres est la plus grande ville d'Angleterre.
   4 Où sont les garçons les moins actifs?
   5 Je prends les vêtements les moins longs.
   6 J'habite dans la région la moins industrielle.

90. Other adjectives

A 1 ce pantalon   2 cet imperméable
   3 cette robe   4 ces baskets
   5 cet anorak   6 ces sandales
   7 ces chaussettes   8 cette jupe

B 1 Je préfère celui à gauche.
   2 Je préfère ceux à gauche.
   3 Je préfère celle à gauche.
   4 Je préfère celles à gauche.

C 1 Quel stylo préfères-tu? Celui-ci ou celui-là?
   2 Quelle station balnéaire préfères-tu? Celle-ci ou celle-là?
   3 Quelles ceintures préfères-tu? Celles-ci ou celles-là?
   4 Quels hôtels préfères-tu? Ceux-ci ou ceux-là?

D 1 Lequel? **2** Laquelle?
 3 Lesquelles? **4** Lesquels?

E 1 Quelle cuisine préfères-tu? Celle-ci ou celle-là? Laquelle?
 2 Quelles cravates préfères-tu? Celles-ci ou celles-là? Lesquelles?
 3 Quel jardin préfères-tu? Celui-ci ou celui-là? Lequel?
 4 Quels gants préfères-tu? Ceux-ci ou ceux-là? Lesquels?

91. Adverbs

A 1 doucement **2** naturellement
 3 absolument **4** généralement
 5 attentivement **6** vraiment
 7 lentement **8** gentiment

B Le matin, <u>d'abord</u> je me lève à sept heures, <u>puis</u> <u>d'habitude</u> je prends mon petit déjeuner. <u>Ensuite</u>, je quitte la maison et <u>finalement</u> j'arrive au collège à huit heures et demie. Mais c'est <u>souvent</u> trop tôt. <u>Alors</u> <u>à l'avenir</u> je vais rester au lit plus longtemps.

In the morning, first of all I get up at 7 o'clock then usually I have my breakfast. Then I leave the house and finally I arrive at school at half past eight. But it is often too early. So, in the future I am going to stay in bed longer.

C Souvent mes grands-parents viennent avec nous, et d'abord c'est vraiment pratique car ils font régulièrement du baby-sitting. Cependant, de temps en temps, ils se sentent vraiment fatigués et ils ne sont pas toujours confortables. Par conséquent ils ne viendront pas l'année prochaine. À l'avenir, ils viendront seulement s'ils sont absolument en bonne forme!

D 2 D'habitude il fait la vaisselle tout de suite.
 3 De temps en temps elle écoute de la musique doucement.
 4 Ma valise? Naturellement j'avais laissé mes vêtements dedans.

92. Object pronouns

A 1 We see you. **2** Do you know him?
 3 I want to see her. **4** You meet us.
 5 She will forget you. **6** I will lose them.

B 1 I am passing my sweets to you.
 2 Do not tell the truth to him *or* to her.
 3 We will give a boat to him/to her.
 4 He is going to send us a present.
 5 You will tell them the story.

C 1 Vous comprenez le professeur? Nous le comprenons souvent.
 2 Elle aime les sports nautiques? Elle ne les aime pas du tout.
 3 Tu vas vendre ton vélo? Oui, je vais le vendre demain.
 4 Il veut acheter la maison? Non, il ne veut pas l'acheter.

D 1 Il les cherche.
 2 Nous lui envoyons un cadeau. / Nous l'envoyons à Jeanne.
 3 Il leur a donné des bonbons. / Il les a donnés aux enfants.
 4 Tu leur as téléphoné?
 5 Elle la dit toujours à papa. / Elle lui dit toujours la vérité.

E 1 Elle nous les a offerts.
 2 Ne les lui vends pas!
 3 Je vais te *or* vous le passer.
 4 Il te *or* vous les a donnés samedi.

93. Other pronouns: *y* and *en*

A 1 Il va y habiter.
 2 Elle y a vu ses amis.
 3 Vous y jouez?
 4 J'y ai réussi.
 5 Tu y es allée ce matin?

B 1 J'en fais beaucoup.
 2 Elle n'en fait pas.
 3 Non, j'en ai trois.
 4 Ils en mangent tous les samedis.
 5 Il y en a plusieurs.

C 1 J'y vais de temps en temps.
 2 … j'en mange beaucoup.
 3 … je n'en mange jamais …
 4 J'y suis allé …
 5 … tu veux y aller …
 6 … mon frère n'en mange pas …

94. Other pronouns

A 1 Le repas que j'ai pris était excellent.
 2 C'est Claude qui est le plus beau.
 3 Ce sont mes parents qui adorent la viande.
 4 Voilà le chapeau qu'il a perdu.
 5 Où sont les robes qui sont déchirées?
 6 L'église que j'ai visitée était vieille.
 7 L'homme qui monte dans le train est gros.
 8 Ma copine qui s'appelle Mathilde a seize ans.
 9 Quel est le film que tu veux voir?

B 1 The life which you are dreaming about does not exist.
 2 The papers which I need are in the drawer.
 3 I do not know the illness from which you are suffering.
 4 This boy who I was talking to you about, has left the school.

C 1 Le repas que nous avons mangé était excellent. = The meal which we ate was excellent.
 2 Le stylo dont vous avez besoin est cassé. = The pen that you need is broken.
 3 Des bonbons? J'en ai mangé beaucoup. = Sweets? I have eaten lots of them.
 4 Le café où je vais le samedi est fermé. = The café where I go on Saturdays is closed.

5 Le cinéma Gaumont? J'y suis allée pour voir 'Amélie'. = The Gaumont cinema? I went there to see 'Amelie'.

95. Present tense: -ER verbs

A **aimer:** j'aime, nous aimons, ils aiment

jouer: je joue, nous jouons, ils jouent

habiter: j'habite, nous habitons, ils habitent

regarder: je regarde, nous regardons, ils regardent

donner: je donne, nous donnons, ils donnent

inviter: j'invite, nous invitons, ils invitent

marcher: je marche, nous marchons, ils marchent

trouver: je trouve, nous trouvons, ils trouvent

voler: je vole, nous volons, ils volent

garder: je garde, nous gardons, ils gardent

B **1** vous gardez   **2** elle invite
3 tu habites   **4** nous trouvons
5 il regarde   **6** vous marchez
7 tu donnes   **8** elle vole
9 il joue   **10** ils regardent

C *-ger* **verbs:**
1 ils rangent   **2** nous plongeons
3 nous nageons   **4** je mange
-yer **verbs:**
5 tu envoies   **6** vous payez
7 j'essaie   **8** nous nettoyons
-ler / -ter **verbs:**
1 je m'appelle   **2** ils jettent
3 nous nous rappelons   **4** elle projette
acheter **type verbs: 5** tu achètes
6 elles préfèrent   **7** vous vous levez
8 il gèle

D **1** Ils habitent en France? Do they live in France?
2 Marie range sa chambre? Does Marie tidy her room?
3 Vous préférez les sciences? Do you prefer science?
4 Les sœurs jettent les fruits? Do the sisters throw out the fruit?
5 Mon copain et moi achetons des frites? Are my friend and I buying chips?

96. -IR and -RE verbs

A choisir = to choose
réfléchir = to think about
ralentir = to slow down
rougir = to blush
finir = to finish
punir = to punish
atterrir = to land
avertir = to warn

B

	dormir	sortir
je	**dors**	sors
tu	dors	**sors**
il / elle	**dort**	sort
nous	**dormons**	**sortons**
vous	**dormez**	sortez
ils	dorment	**sortent**

C **1** L'ami choisit un cadeau.
2 Vous courez aux magasins.
3 Nous finissons nos devoirs.
4 Je remplis le verre de vin.

D

	vendre	prendre	dire
je	**vends**	**prends**	**dis**
tu	vends	**prends**	**dis**
il / elle	**vend**	**prend**	**dit**
nous	**vendons**	prenons	disons
vous	**vendez**	prenez	dites
ils / elles	vendent	**prennent**	**disent**

E **1** nous vendons   **2** ils répondent
3 je descends   **4** tu prends
5 vous buvez   **6** elle lit
7 j'écris   **8** il comprend

97. *avoir* and *être*

A **1** Elle a un hamster.
2 J'ai les cheveux blonds.
3 Ils ont une grande maison.
4 Il a onze ans.
5 Nous avons un petit gymnase.
6 Vous avez un beau chien.
7 Ma sœur a une jupe rouge.
8 Les filles ont un piercing.
9 Tu as deux guitares.
10 Vous avez une nouvelle maison.

B **1** Ils ont un chien et trois hamsters.
2 Tu as une sœur?
3 Elle a les cheveux noirs.
4 Nous avons une grande cuisine.
5 J'ai trois enfants.
6 J'ai seize ans.
7 Il a une voiture.

C 1 Je suis français.
  2 Nous sommes paresseux.
  3 Ma tante est assez petite.
  4 Vous êtes sportif mais timide.
  5 Mes yeux sont bleus.
  6 Tu es célibataire?
  7 Les chiens sont mignons.
  8 Je suis au chômage.
  9 Nous sommes mariés.
  10 Il est paresseux.

98. *aller* and *faire*

A 1 Les jeunes vont au centre commercial.
  2 Je vais au marché samedi.
  3 Vous allez sortir ce soir?
  4 Maman va à l'église.
  5 Où vas-tu vendredi soir?
  6 Les chiens vont dans le garage.
  7 Les parents vont au restaurant.
  8 Marc va au centre sportif.
  9 Nous allons en France pour nos vacances.
  10 Je vais au collège.

B 1 Mon frère fait la vaisselle. = My brother does the dishes.
  2 Mes sœurs font tout le ménage. = My sisters do all the housework.
  3 Vous faites le repassage. = You do the ironing.
  4 Nous faisons la cuisine. = We do the cooking.
  5 Ils font le jardinage. = They do the gardening.
  6 Je fais la lessive. = I do the (clothes) washing.
  7 Maman fait les courses = Mum does the shopping.
  8 Tu fais du shopping. = You go shopping.

C 1 Ma sœur fait de la danse.
  2 Nous faisons des randonnées.
  3 Ils font du ski nautique.
  4 Tu fais de la gymnastique.
  5 Vous faites de la danse?
  6 Elles font de l'équitation.
  7 Nous faisons de la planche à voile.
  8 Il fait de l'escalade.

D 1 Jean va à la pêche.
  2 Nous faisons de la voile tous les samedis.
  3 Vous faites du basket.
  4 Ils vont à la montagne pour faire du ski.
  5 Tu vas au concert avec moi?
  6 Ils font de l'athlétisme.
  7 Elle va souvent au cinéma.
  8 Je vais faire des promenades.
  9 Tu fais du skate?
  10 Mes camarades font du vélo.

99. Modal verbs

A

	devoir	pouvoir	vouloir	savoir
je	dois	**peux**	**veux**	sais
tu	**dois**	peux	**veux**	**sais**
il / elle /on	**doit**	peut	veut	sait
nous	devons	**pouvons**	**voulons**	savons
vous	**devez**	pouvez	voulez	**savez**
ils / elles	**doivent**	peuvent	**veulent**	savent

B 1 Pouvez-vous aider mon père?
  2 Sais-tu nager?
  3 Mes parents veulent acheter une nouvelle maison.
  4 On doit toujours s'arrêter aux feux rouges.
  5 Voulez-vous danser avec moi ce soir?
  6 Je sais parler allemand et français.

C 1 nous voulons trouver une chambre avec un balcon
  2 tu peux louer un vélo
  3 vous devez tout vérifier
  4 ils savent faire la cuisine
  5 elles peuvent faire un pique-nique
  6 vous ne pouvez jamais comprendre les régles
  7 je sais préparer le dîner

D *Examples*: On ne doit pas manger en classe. On ne veut pas répondre aux professeurs. On peut dormir en classe. On ne sait pas envoyer des textos.

100. Reflexive verbs

A Je me lève / Tu te laves / Il se brosse les dents / Je m'habille et après / Je prends mon petit déjeuner

B Mes parents SE réveillent tôt le matin. Je m'appelle Lydie. Le matin je me réveille à 7 heures et demie mais je ne me lève pas tout de suite. Normalement ma sœur se lève à 8 heures. Nous nous lavons dans la salle de bains et nous nous habillons vite. Après le petit déjeuner, nous nous dépêchons pour prendre le bus au collège. On s'approche du collège et on est très contentes. Vous vous amusez bien à votre collège?

C 2, 1, 4, 3

D 1 je me repose   je me suis reposé(e)
  2 elle se douche   elle s'est douchée
  3 nous nous amusons   nous nous sommes amusé(e)s
  4 elles s'étonnent   elles se sont étonnées
  5 vous vous dépêchez   vous vous êtes dépêché(e)(s)

E 1 Je me suis reposée à 8 heures ce matin.
   2 Nous nous sommes dépêchés pour aller au match.
   3 Ma sœur ne s'est pas douchée hier soir.
   4 Mes deux frères se sont bien entendus en vacances.
   5 Vous vous êtes couchés tôt samedi, mes amis?
   6 Les garçons se sont disputés.

101. The perfect tense 1

A *Examples:* J'ai vendu la maison. Elle a détesté le bateau. Nous avons fini les devoirs.

B 1 Mme Le Blanc a invité sa copine au match.
   2 Vous avez terminé le repas?
   3 Ils ont fumé une cigarette.
   4 Il a beaucoup neigé ce matin.
   5 Tu n'as pas mangé de légumes?
   6 Nous avons choisi un bon restaurant.
   7 Elle n'a pas rougi.
   8 Ils ont atterri à l'aéroport d'Orly.
   9 J'ai rendu visite à ma tante.
   10 Nous n'avons pas entendu.

C 1 Nous n'avons pas perdu l'argent.
   2 Ils n'ont pas lavé le bus.
   3 Vous n'avez pas attendu les chiens.
   4 Je n'ai pas fini le pain.
   5 Elle n'a pas vendu le bateau.
   6 Il n'a pas détesté les devoirs.

D 1 J'ai mis le pique-nique par terre.
   2 Elle a écrit à son frère.
   3 Tu n'as rien fait au collège?
   4 Il n'a pas lu ma lettre.
   5 Nous avons pu acheter une Renault.

E 1 J'ai compris la situation.
   2 Il a promis de rentrer vite.
   3 Tu as pris un taxi à la gare?
   4 Qu'est-ce que tu as fait?

102. The perfect tense 2

A 1 Elle est tombée par terre.
   2 Mes copains sont arrivés trop tard.
   3 Les chats sont montés sur le toit.
   4 Marie n'est pas descendue vite.
   5 Madame Lebrun est allée à la piscine.
   6 Vous êtes retournés en France?
   7 Je ne suis pas parti tôt.
   8 Elles sont mortes l'année dernière.

B 1 Élise est arrivée à 11 heures.
   2 Jim est mort il y a 20 ans.
   3 Nous sommes entrés dans l'épicerie.
   4 Marie n'est rentrée qu'à minuit.
   5 Mes stylos ne sont pas tombés.
   6 Il est sorti avec sa sœur jumelle.

C 1 elles sont montées très vite
   2 je suis arrivé(e)
   3 ils ne sont pas tombés
   4 elle est morte

D je me suis lavé(e)   tu t'es lavé(e)
   il s'est lavé   elle s'est lavée
   nous nous sommes lavé(e)(s)
   vous vous êtes lavé(e)(s)
   ils se sont lavés   ells se sont lavées

E 1 Hier soir nous nous sommes couchés tôt.
   2 Ils ne se sont pas bien amusés au parc.
   3 Elle s'est ennuyée au collège ce matin.

F 1 Ils se sont couchés.
   2 Elle s'est ennuyée.
   3 Vous vous êtes disputé(e)(s).
   4 Je me suis endormi(e).

103. The imperfect tense

A 1 **jouer**
      je jouais
      nous jouions
      ils jouaient
   2 **finir**
      je finissais
      nous finissions
      ils finissaient
   3 **perdre**
      je perdais
      nous perdions
      ils perdaient
   4 **avoir**
      j'avais
      nous avions
      ils avaient
   5 **être**
      j'étais
      nous étions
      ils étaient
   6 **boire**
      je buvais
      nous buvions
      ils buvaient
   7 **aller**
      j'allais
      nous allions
      ils allaient
   8 **partir**
      je partais
      nous partions
      ils partaient
   9 **faire**
      je faisais
      nous faisions
      ils faisaient
   10 **lire**
      je lisais
      nous lisions
      ils lisaient
   11 **savoir**
      je savais
      nous savions
      ils savaient

12 prendre
je prenais
nous prenions
ils prenaient

B 1 elle attendait   **2** ils écrivaient
    3 il dormait   **4** je regardais
    5 elles étaient polies

C 1 Je jouais avec mon petit frère sur la plage. = I used to play with my little brother on the beach.
    2 Nous mangions ensemble très souvent. = we used to eat together very often.
    3 Le serveur travaillait dur pour nous. = The waiter used to work hard for us.
    4 On vendait beaucoup de glaces. = They used to sell lots of ice-cream.
    5 Papa et Marc faisaient du ski nautique. = Papa and Marc used to water ski.
    6 Tu étais très content. = You used to be very happy.

D J'allais au collège quand j'ai vu l'accident. Il y avait beaucoup de monde. J'ai appelé «au secours!».

104. The future tense

A 1 Il va sortir ce soir. = He is going to go out this evening.
    2 Nous allons vendre la maison. = We are going to sell the house.
    3 Vous allez comprendre bientôt. = You are going to understand soon.
    4 Tu vas partir en vacances. = You are going to go away on holiday.
    5 Maman va voir un concert. = Mum is going to see a concert.
    6 Les garçons vont arriver en retard. = The boys are going to arrive late.

B 1 Nous allons aller en ville demain.
    2 Quand vas-tu partir?
    3 Ils vont faire leurs devoirs.
    4 Vous allez jouer au tennis?
    5 Lydie va faire la cuisine.
    6 Ses sœurs vont aider.

C 1 Il lavera sa nouvelle voiture.
    2 Tu inviteras ta copine à manger.
    3 Nous finirons nos devoirs.
    4 Vous attendrez les nouvelles.
    5 Elle rendra visite à sa grand-mère.
    6 Ils arriveront en France.
    7 Elles bavarderont beaucoup.
    8 Je choisirai une nouvelle robe.

D 1 ils devront   **2** nous saurons
    3 je ferai   **4** elle sera
    5 tu auras   **6** elles viendront
    7 il verra   **8** tu iras

E 1 they will have to   **2** we will know
    3 I will do   **4** she will be
    5 you will have   **6** they will come
    7 he will see   **8** you will go

105. The conditional

A

	-er verbs	-ir verbs	-re verbs
	jouer	choisir	vendre
je	jouerais	**choisirais**	**vendrais**
tu	**jouerais**	choisirais	**vendrais**
il / elle	**jouerait**	**choisirait**	vendrait
nous	**jouerions**	choisirions	**vendrions**
vous	joueriez	**choisiriez**	vendriez
ils / elles	**joueraient**	choisiraient	**vendraient**

B 1 Ma mère habiterait une belle maison. = My mum would live in a beautiful house.
    2 Vous ne travailleriez plus. = You would no longer work.
    3 Nous visiterions beaucoup de pays. = We would visit lots of countries.
    4 Tu offrirais de l'argent aux autres. = You would give money to others.
    5 Ils mettraient de l'argent à la banque. = They would put some money in the bank.
    6 Je vendrais ma vieille voiture. = I would sell my old car.

C 1 Je serais très riche.
    2 Vous verriez le monde entier.
    3 Ils auraient beaucoup d'amis.
    4 Elle voudrait épouser son fiancé.

106. The pluperfect tense

A 1 You had already finished your lunch.
    2 We had heard the news.
    3 They had promised to return before midnight.
    4 You had already drunk the whole bottle.
    5 She had never read this book.
    6 They had already left.
    7 She had come on her own.
    8 The children had gone to bed early.

B 1 Elle avait fini.
    2 Nous avions lu.
    3 Elles étaient arrivées.
    4 Vous étiez partis.
    5 Tu étais tombé?

C 1 **c:** I had always wanted to go to Bordeaux but my parents decided to go to Alsace.
    2 **a:** He had gone on holiday when we arrived at the house.
    3 **f:** They had left when it started to rain.
    4 **e:** Luckily, we had bought some sandwiches.
    5 **d:** My sister had left early but there was a lot of traffic.
    6 **g:** My parents had rented a flat by the seaside.
    7 **h:** If you had won the lottery, what would you have done?
    8 **b:** I had left my car in the car park.

107. Negatives

A ne … pas = not
ne … jamais = never
ne … plus = no longer, no more
ne … rien = nothing, not anything
ne … personne = nobody, not anybody
ne … aucun = not any, none
ne … que = only
ne … ni … ni = neither … nor
ne … pas encore = not yet

B 1 We like neither geography nor history.
2 I will no longer eat any meat.
3 He never arrived.
4 They found nothing.
5 I am sending no postcards.
6 She only does two hours per month.
7 He will never return to Italy again.

C 1 Nous n'avons aucune idée.
2 Paul n'a que dix euros.
3 Personne n'est venu à ma fête.
4 Ils n'ont rien bu au café.
5 Vous n'achèterez plus de chocolat?

D 1 Nous ne fumerons plus de cigarettes.
2 Elle n'a jamais dit bonjour.
3 Tu ne rencontres que deux amies en ville.
4 Il n'a rien compris.

E 1 Non, ils n'ont jamais acheté de maison.
2 Non, elle n'a pas fait de lecture.
3 Non, elles ne sont jamais venues.

108. Questions

A 1 Est-ce qu'il peut venir lundi?
2 Est-ce que vous avez une carte de la ville?
3 Est-ce que les élèves ont fini leurs devoirs?
4 Est-ce qu'elle veut aller en ville?
5 Est-ce que vous êtes vendeuse?
6 Est-ce que nous arriverons au collège à l'heure?

B 1 C 2 D 3 E 4 B 5 A

C Est-ce que tu vas en ville demain matin?
Est-ce qu'il joue au tennis?
Est-ce qu'elle partira en vacances en juillet?
Est-ce que tu as perdu ta clef?
Est-ce que tu as réservé une chambre?
Est-ce que tu préfères voyager en avion ou par le train?
Est-ce que les portables sont utiles?
Est-ce que le chien est mignon?
Est-ce que tu veux aller au cinéma avec moi?
Est-ce que tu sais faire de la voile?

D 1 B 2 H 3 D 4 E 5 A
6 G 7 F 8 C

E *Example questions:* Où habites-tu? À quelle heure est-ce que tu te lèves le matin? Combien de frères est-ce que tu as? Qu'est-ce que tu aimes faire le weekend?

109. Useful little words

A 1 F 2 G 3 H 4 B 5 D
6 C 7 E 8 A

B far from, near to, opposite
in front of, behind, beside
nowhere, everywhere, for or against
on the right, on the left, about

C D'abord, je me suis levée à 7 heures, puis je me suis lavée. Je suis entrée dans la salle de bains, située près de ma chambre et j'ai décidé de prendre une douche et de me brosser les dents aussi. Après ma douche, j'ai cherché ma serviette partout. Mais je ne l'ai trouvée nulle part. À la fin j'ai réussi à retrouver ma serviette parmi mes affaires et je suis rentrée dans ma chambre.

First of all, I got up at 7 o'clock then I had a wash. I went in to the bathroom, situated near my bedroom and I decided to take a shower and brush my teeth as well. After my shower, I looked for my towel everywhere. But I found it nowhere. In the end I managed to find my towel amongst my things and I went back into my bedroom.

D 1 donc 2 ensuite 3 aussi
4 partout 5 mais 6 pendant
7 avant 8 en face de 9 chez
10 parmi 11 devant 12 près de
13 environ 14 sans 15 vers

110. Useful bits and pieces

A 1 vendredi 2 automne
3 mercredi 4 hiver 5 lundi
6 samedi 7 dimanche 8 été
9 printemps 10 jeudi 11 mardi

B 1 La Saint-Sylvestre, c'est le trente-et-un décembre.
2 Pâques, c'est le huit avril.
3 Le Nouvel An, c'est le premier janvier.
4 la fête nationale, c'est le quatorze juillet.

C (a) treize
(b) seize
(c) vingt-et-un
(d) vingt-cinq
(e) trente-sept
(f) quarante-trois
(g) cinquante-neuf
(h) soixante-quatre
(i) soixante-et-onze
(j) quatre-vingt-quatre
(k) quatre-vingt-douze
(l) cent

D **1** B **2** F **3** A **4** C **5** E **6** D

E **1** Je voudrais un demi kilo de cerises.
  2 Je voudrais une bouteille de lait.
  3 Je voudrais un morceau de fromage.
  4 Je voudrais 4 tranches de jambon.
  5 Je voudrais une boîte de sardines.
  6 Je voudrais une cannette de limonade.
  7 Je voudrais un pot de confiture.
  8 Je voudrais cinq livres de pommes de terre.

Practice Exam Paper

111. Reading

1 **(a)** E **(b)** D **(c)** F **(d)** B
  (e) J **(f)** H

2 **(a)** B **(b)** G **(c)** F **(d)** D

3 **(a)** B **(b)** A **(c)** C **(d)** A
  (e) B

4 Carole: Advantage: (made) new friends *(1)*
Disadvantage: tired (in the evening) *(1)*

Delphine: Advantage: no toothache *(1)*
Disadvantage: started to smoke *(1)*

5 **(a)** L **(b)** Q **(c)** B **(d)** B
  (e) Q **(f)** L **(g)** L

6 **(a)** P/N **(b)** P **(c)** N
  (d) P **(e)** P/N **(f)** N

7 D, F, H, I, J *(in any order)*

8 **(a)** unemployment
  (b) **(i)** has been unemployed for 10 years
    (ii) not finding a job *(2)*
  (c) grow food
  (d) to avoid the heat
  (e) **(i)** the school was given equipment
    (ii) he can do research on a computer *(2)*
  (f) be a doctor

9 **(a)** A **(b)** L **(c)** E **(d)** F
  (e) C **(f)** I **(g)** K **(h)** H

117. Listening

1 **(i)** black **(ii)** small **(iii)** blue
  (iv) shy **(v)** lazy **(vi)** purple / violet

2 **1** C **2** E **3** B **4** F

3 **1** B 6 *(2)* **2** C 4 *(2)* **3** D 5 *(2)*

4 **1** Advantage: colleagues nice / pleasant *(1)* /
Disadvantage: tiring *(1)*
  2 Advantage: well paid *(1)* / Disadvantage: hours too long *(1)*
  3 Advantage: gets money off *(1)* / Disadvantage: boring *(1)*

5 **1** P/N **2** P **3** P/N
  4 N **5** N

6 **1** H, G *(2)* **2** E, I *(2)* **3** F, B *(2)*

7 **1** A **2** C **3** B **4** C

8 **(a)** 45%
  (b) **(i)** to be greener / more eco-friendly **(ii)** high price of petrol *(2)*
  (c) travel by plane
  (d) **(i)** bought organic products **(ii)** not bought products with too much packaging **(iii)** cleaned a river *(3)*
  (e) left rubbish on beach
  (f) dog cut itself on (discarded) can

9 **Part 1:** D, E, H *(in any order)*
Part 2: C, D, F *(in any order)*

Published by Pearson Education Limited, 80 Strand, London, WC2R 0RL.

www.pearsonschoolsandfecolleges.co.uk

Text © Pearson Education Limited 2013
Audio recorded at Tom Dick + Debbie Productions, © Pearson Education Limited
MFL Series Editor: Julie Green
Edited by Patricia Dunn and Sue Chapple
Typeset by Kamae Design, Oxford
Original illustrations © Pearson Education Limited 2013
Illustrations by KJA Artists and John Hallett
Cover illustration by Miriam Sturdee

The rights of Stuart Glover and Janet Calderbank to be identified as authors of this work
have been asserted by them in accordance with the Copyright, Designs and Patents Act
1988.

The authors and publishers are grateful to Suzanne Hilton and Martin Bradley for the use
of some original material.

First published 2013

16 15
10 9 8 7

British Library Cataloguing in Publication Data
A catalogue record for this book is available from the British Library

ISBN 978 1 447 94106 4

Printed in Slovakia by Neografia

In the writing of this book, no AQA examiners authored sections relevant to examination
papers for which they have responsibility.